depending on their aspirations and e<
fundamental changes that were takir
in the form it took, was not inevitabl

Chris Fisher originally worke<
moving to Britain to study at W
completing his MA in Comparati..
History, Fisher gained a PhD in Social History in 1978 with ms u.....
Free Miners and Colliers: Custom, the Crown and Trade Unionism in the Forest of Dean, 1788-1886, which became a book *Custom, Work and Market Capitalism. The Forest of Dean Colliers, 1788-1888*, published by Croom Helm in 1981. The first chapters of *Custom, Work and Market Capitalism* discuss the causes of the riot in more detail with an account of how the ownership and the use of resources in the Forest between the years 1788 – 1886 were fundamentally transformed in ways which favoured private property, the exchange of commodities for profit, and the accumulation for a few at the expense of the labouring many.

Fisher returned to Australia in 1978. In subsequent years he held teaching posts at the Universities of Wollongong, New South Wales and Canberra, and research posts with the Australasian Coal and Shale Employees Federation, the Industrial Relations Research Centre at the University of New South Wales, the Research School of Social Sciences at the Australian National University and the Australian Public Service. He has published several books and articles about labour history and industrial relations. In the years between 1986 and 2018, Fisher worked as a grain and sheep farmer at Temora in New South Wales. He is now retired.

In 1986 Ralph Anstis published *Warren James and Dean Forest Riots* (Coleford, self-published) which has become the most popular and widely read account of the events surrounding the 1831 riot. In the second part of his book, Anstis provides a detailed account of the trial of the rioters and Warren James' imprisonment, transportation to Tasmania, ill-treatment and finally death at the age of 49 in 1841.[1]

Both Anstis's and Fisher's books became out of print and difficult to source and so Breviary Publications reprinted *Warren James and Dean Forest Riots* in 2011 and *Custom, Work and Market Capitalism* in 2016.

Ian Wright, Autumn 2020

1 Further details and original documents have been compiled by Terry James and can be accessed from the Forest of Dean Family History Society website under Stories and Articles, Riots in the Forest of Dean 1831. https://forest-of-dean.net

Preface

The Royal Forest of Dean lies in western Gloucestershire, in the wedge formed by the lower reaches of the Rivers Severn and Wye. The Forest in 1831 comprised an area of about 24,000 acres of extra-parochial Crown land which, together with some surrounding parishes, made up the old administrative division of the Hundred of St Briavels.[2] It is the central area of Crown land with which this paper is concerned. The Forest was rich in natural resources including timber, iron ore, limestone and coal which had supported, from perhaps before Roman times, several industries including iron ore mining and iron making. In 1831, however, coal mining was the largest employer of men in the Forest.

In June 1831, the coal miners rioted and broke down enclosures which the Crown had made in the Forest in 1810. The purpose of this paper is to ask why they did so? The few references which have been made to the event in secondary sources describe it as an anti-enclosure riot. This paper will argue, however, that the riot was a much more complex affair than that. It will contend that it was the product of conflicts of interest generated after 1800 in the assertion by the Crown of its rights in the Forest and the related penetration of, and transformation of, the old 'free mining' coal industry by capitalists from beyond the borders of Dean.

2 St Briavels was an ancient hundred of Gloucestershire. It comprised the extra-parochial area of the Forest of Dean, and the ancient parishes of Abenhall, English Bicknor, St Briavels, Littledean, Flaxley, Hewelsfield, Mitcheldean, Newland, Ruardean, Staunton and Lea (part). The hundred was created at some time between 1086 and 1220 to provide a structure for the administration of the Forest of Dean. The meeting place was St Briavels Castle. An extra-parochial area was a geographically defined area considered to be outside any ecclesiastical or civil parish. They had no church or clergymen and were therefore exempt from payment of poor or church rates and usually tithes. They were formed for a variety of reasons, often because an area was unpopulated or unsuitable for agriculture such as woodlands and commons.

Bristol Radical Pamphleteer #50

The Forest of Dean Miners' Riot of 1831

Chris Fisher

ISBN 978-1-911522-56-0

Bristol Radical History Group. 2020.
www.brh.org.uk
brh@brh.org.uk

Contents

Preface to BRHG Edition

The Forest of Dean uprising of 1831 received scant attention from historians before 1975 when Chris Fisher started researching the subject as part of his MA in history studies at the University of Warwick. His MA dissertation was the first thorough study of the riot and is up to now unpublished. BRHG decided to publish it in its original form as we believe that it provides an alternative and critical insight into the events surrounding 1831.

Fisher argues that the Forest of Dean Riot of 1831 was fundamentally a miners' riot. He contends that it was the product of conflicts of interest generated after 1800 in the assertion by the State of its claim to rights in the Forest of Dean and the related penetration and transformation of the old free mining coal industry by capitalists from beyond the borders of the Forest. His analysis of the changes in mine ownership reveals that in the years between 1790 and 1830 the mining industry in the Forest of Dean had passed, in the main, from the hands of a relatively large group of working proprietors of small scale co-operative pits into those of a small group of men, mostly outside capitalists, who brought with them the steam engine, deep mining, railroads and iron furnaces. As a result, most of the inhabitants of the Forest became wage earners.

Fisher's discussion of land use, encroachments and the construction of enclosures reveals that the inhabitants' opportunities to use the Forest for timber stealing, pasture and cottages had also been curtailed. Tensions were exacerbated by a growing population and an influx of foreign workmen.

Fisher argues that three factors were of critical importance in the processes which brought about these changes: the determination of the State to reassert its control; the expediency for the State of an alliance with outside capitalists; and the willingness of some free miners to take on outside capitalists as partners.

Fisher backs his arguments up with critical use of primary sources and accounts of the riot, which often represent differing points of view. In doing so he challenges the view presented by some at the time that the rioters were misguided, naïve, ignorant, simple and deluded. On the contrary, Fisher contends that the riot was a clear expression of considerable and justifiable resentment towards the State and the foreign capitalists as they encroached on the free miners' control of the Forest's resources. However, he argues the situation was complex as different free miners responded in a variety of ways to the changing circumstances

Maps

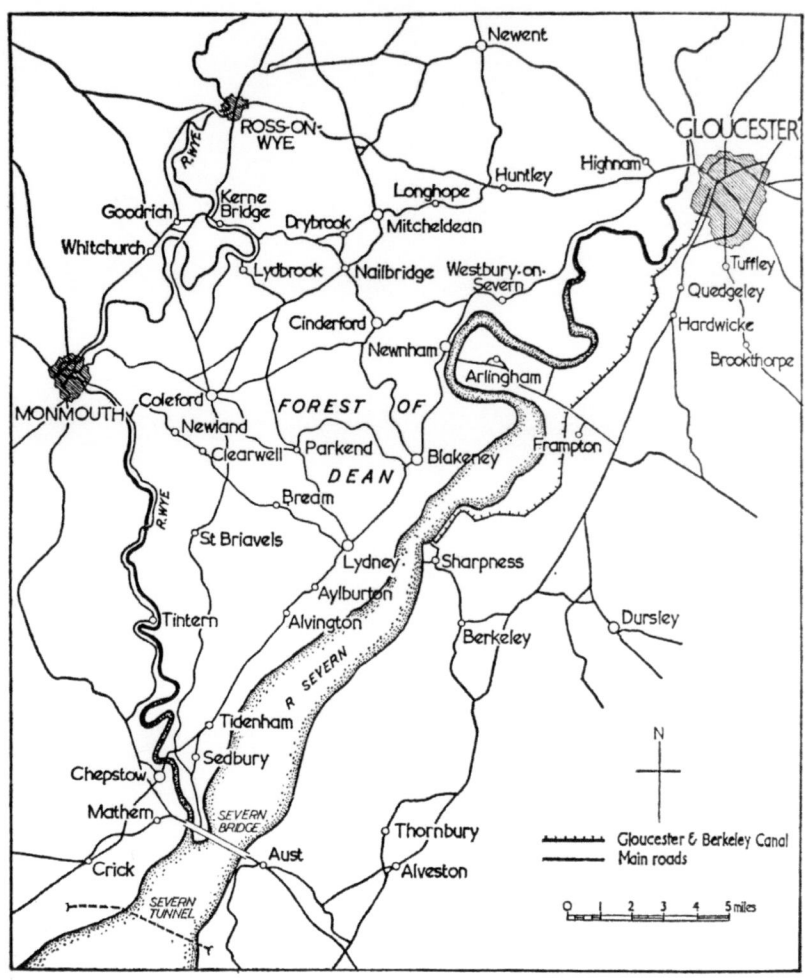

The Forest of Dean and its neighbourhood.

Reproduced from C E Hart, *The Industrial History of Dean* (Newton Abbot, David and Charles, 1971) xxviii.

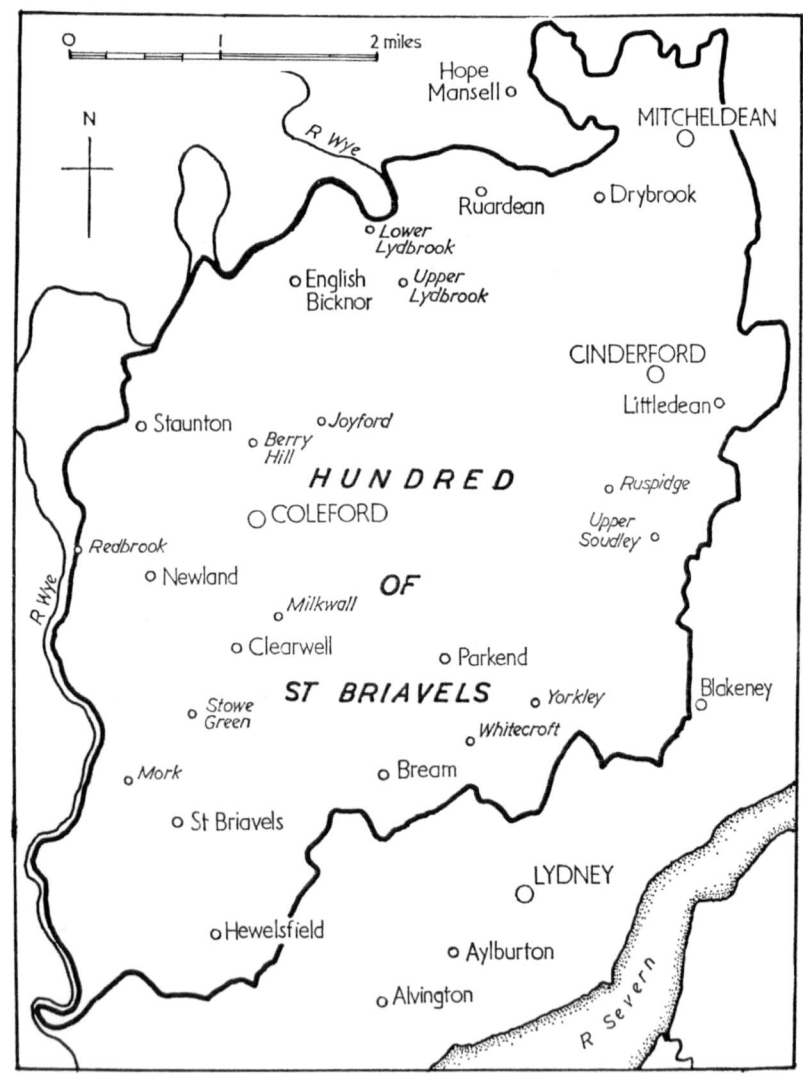

The Hundred of St Briavels.

Reproduced from C E Hart, *The Industrial History of Dean* (Newton Abbot, David and Charles, 1971) 224.

Introduction

This paper will attempt to explain why it was that the Forest of Dean miners rioted in June 1831. This riot has so far not been given the attention it deserves by historians. In their "Table of Incidents" for 1830-31, Hobsbawm and Rude listed it as a "poorhouse riot".[3] Whatever poorhouse riots may have been, this paper should make it clear that the Dean riot was not one of them. In another place Rude has classified the riot as part of the agricultural labourers' movement of 1830-31 and as one of "a handful of enclosure riots".[4] The local historian Hart also described the Dean riot as "a local anti-enclosure movement".[5] Certainly, the immediate objective of the riot was the destruction of enclosures which the Crown had made in the Forest to protect young plantations of trees. However, this paper will argue, the matter was a good deal more complex than that.

The riot marked a stage in the transformation of the 'free mining' district of Dean by the joint pressures of, on the one hand, capital and the modes of industrial organisation and the notions of property which went with it and, on the other, the demands of an intrusive State, concerned to redefine old use rights in the Forest in the light of the 'public interest'. For most of the eighteenth century, the miners in Dean sheltered behind the ancient 'Laws and Customs' of the Free Miners and their Mine Law Court. The industry was conducted on a small scale by native owner-miners who jealously guarded their interests against outsiders, or 'foreigners' defined as people who had been born outside of the Hundred of St Briavels. The laxity of the State's administration of the Forest allowed men to combine mining with small landholding and other uses of the Forest's resources.

However, by 1831, most free miners had become wage labourers, the Mine Law Court had disappeared and the industry had passed, in the main, under the control of 'foreign' capitalists. The Forest's administrators, under the pressure of 'economical reform' in central government, had severely curtailed the uses people could make of the Forest. The processes which brought about a capitalist reorganisation of mining and revived the State's administrative control began towards

---

3 E J Hobsbawm and G Rude, *Captain Swing* (Revised edition, London: Penguin, 1973) Appendix III.
4 G Rude, English Rural and Urban Disturbances on the Eve of the First Reform Bill, 1830-31, *Past and Present*, 37 (1967), 90.
5 C E Hart, *The Royal Forest* (Oxford: Clarendon, 1966).

the end of the eighteenth century and reached a climax in a series of Acts of Parliament between 1835 and 1841. A distinct stage in these developments began about 1828 when the State took steps to limit the miners' rights by legislation. The riot, this paper will argue, was the result of a counter-campaign by the miners in which they, for a variety of reasons, attempted to resist further the erosion of their 'rights' and bring about the restoration of the Mine Law Court, the old customs and the miners' old control of the Forest's resources. The campaign and the riot drew upon and expressed a considerable hostility to and resentment of the foreigners and the State, seen as allies in dispossessing the free miners.

This riot was thus of a kind with those examined by Thompson, Rude, Hobsbawm, Jones and others which mark the resistance of a great variety of people to the re-ordering of ways of living and working by economic and political change in Britain in the eighteenth and early nineteenth centuries.[6] The study of popular disturbances by those historians has provided a means of insight into the nature of change, its consequences for and the part played in it by the 'lower orders'. Contrary to the opinions of some of their predecessors, recent historians have concluded that popular disturbances were not simply impulsive bursts of irrational, violent energy among, principally, the criminal elements of society. Nor were they responses of a Pavlovian directness to the stimulus of hunger. Disciplined, rational and often highly ritualised and stylised, popular disturbances marked the intervention by a wide cross-section of the labouring and artisan population against the processes by which they were governed. Rioters displayed an awareness of, and a concern to influence, the impact of political and economic events on their own lives:[7]

the 'just' price and the 'just' wage, imposed by authority or sanctioned by custom, gave way to the new prevailing notions of 'natural' wages and prices in a freely competitive market.[8]

6 See E J Hobsbawm and G Rude, *Captain Swing*, Revised edition, (London: Penguin, 1973); G Rude, *The Crowd in History*, (New York: Wiley, 1964); E P Thompson, English Trade Unionism and other Labour Movements Before 1790, *Society for the Study of Labour History*, Bulletin, (Autumn, 1968), The Moral Economy of the English Crowd in the Eighteenth Century, *Past and Present*, No.50 (1971) and *The Making of the English Working Class*, (Revised Edition, London: Penguin, 1968), Chapters 3 and 6; see also the introduction to J Stevenson and R Quinault, *Popular Protest and Public Order*, (London: Allen and Unwin, 1974); and D Jones, *Before Rebecca*, (London: Allen Lane, 1973).
7 Rude, *The Crowd in History*, 224.
8 Ibid, 226.

Against the innovators, common people appealed to ancient rights, customs and statute:

> they appealed to Parliament, to magistrates, and to the King himself to restore or enforce the old regulations: to forbid enclosure, to pull down toll gates, to empower justices to fix prices and wages and to regulate the supply and distribution of bread and flour.[9]

"It is possible," Thompson wrote, "to detect in almost every eighteenth-century crowd action some legitimizing notion. By the notion of legitimation, I mean that the men and women in the crowd were informed by the belief that they were defending traditional rights or customs". The crowd believed itself to be "supported by a wider community consensus, a consistent traditional view of social norms and obligations, of the proper economic functions of several parties within the community, which, taken together, can be said to constitute the moral economy of the poor".[10] Jones wrote similarly of the Welsh disturbances of the late eighteenth and early nineteenth centuries:

> those who turned to violence were usually a closely-knit group of people suffering some kind of economic strain and united by a feeling of injustice because of an attack on, or neglect of, their mythical rights and customs. The 'lower orders' proclaimed that they were determined to defend those rights against the tyranny and oppression of merchants, poor law officers, landlords, employers and the government. At the heart of their protests was a sense of humiliation.[11]

It is in this historiographical context that the Dean riot has some general interest. It was a further case of the invocation by a group of men of "ancient rights and privileges" against intruders and innovators. In this case, the appeal was not to a myth but to a code which had been operative in the memory of miners still alive in 1831. We may not, however, without some qualification, see the Dean riot as a direct conflict between the new and the old; between the exploiters and the exploited. It was that in large part. The conflict, however, was between

9 Ibid.
10 Thompson, *The Moral Economy of the English Crowd*, 78.
11 Jones, *Before Rebecca*, 198.

free miners and intruders. The free miners' experience of change had not been uniform and their motives in looking to the restoration of the Mine Law Court were probably not uniform. Some undoubtedly wished to preserve their exclusive rights and privileges as a means of exclusive benefit from the new system. Nonetheless, we may discern in the riot and the events which produced it both the massive reorganisation of the ownership and control of the Forest's resources by the State and capital and, common to all the groups among the free miners, a sense of dispossession and grievance against the dispossessors.

The paper is arranged in five chapters. The first recounts the tale of the riot and argues that the behaviour of the rioters showed evidence of discipline and purpose. It was not, as H.G. Nicholls wrote, "simply an outburst of the excitability to which the Celtic peoples are prone".[12]

Chapter two will consider some of the suggestions which the contemporary reports of the riot offer about the motives and purposes of the rioters. It will argue that there is no evidence that the riot had anything to do with the 1831 elections or that it was the product of political agitation. We may, however, though the evidence is scanty, see that the riot took place in the context of distress and unemployment in the Forest. While that offers an initial set of reasons for the destruction of the enclosures, it does not account for a more general hostility manifested against both the Crown and foreigners or for the use by the rioters of the language of "rights and privileges" to express their grievances.

That raises problems which the following two chapters discuss. Who were the free miners? What were their rights? What had been their situation before the foreigners came? How had the foreigners and the Crown interfered with the miners' rights? Had the foreigners and the Crown acted as allies?

Chapter five will then focus, firstly on the immediate background to the riot and the moves by the State to limit the miners' rights by legislation after 1828 and the miners' response. The chapter then turns to a reconsideration of the riot and attempts to place it in the context of both the long- and short-term influences at work in the Forest.

The form of the paper is largely determined by the nature of the evidence available. The accounts of the riot which survive were written by

---

12 H G Nicholls, *The Forest of Dean*, 2nd edition, edited by C.N. Hart, (Whitestable: David and Charles, 1966, 1st edition 1858) and H G Nicholls, *The Personalities of the Forest of Dean*, (London: John Murray, 1863) 180.

newspaper correspondents, magistrates and an anonymous biographer of the riot's 'captain', Warren James. They agreed that the rioters were silly, deluded, mistaken and misled. Their assessment of the motives and purposes of the rioters seems to have been compounded of ignorance and special pleading. It is necessary, however, to make use of their reports in order to set out the problem with which we are dealing and to discover clues which might lead, via chapters three and four, to more satisfactory judgements. Necessarily there will be some repetition in chapter five of material used in chapters one and two. By then, however, it should be possible to discriminate among the reports of contemporaries and see meaning in them which was not initially evident.

At no stage in this paper is the evidence entirely satisfactory. At some stages, it is decidedly unsatisfactory and we are reduced to speculation. The little statistical evidence about the Forest which is available is crude and allows only of crude treatment and inference. Some of the gaps in the evidence are alarming. Almost nothing survives about the ways in which the mines were worked and the coal marketed. There is nothing of any value about working conditions or wages in the mines. This paper, however, does not pretend to be a social and economic history of the Forest of Dean, or even of the mining industry. While the weakness or absence of evidence imposes a form of selection on the matters to be discussed here, there is a further limitation in that the paper is narrowly focussed on the riot and the central issue of the ownership and control of the Forest's resources.

Chapter One

Levelling and Enclosures

In June 1831, the miners of the Forest of Dean rioted. Over four days, led by their captain Warren James, they held control of the Forest, defied the authority of the resident officers of the Crown and did considerable damage to the property of the Crown. Not intimidated by a small party of soldiers from Monmouth, they scattered to hide in the woods and coal pits only when confronted by the Third Dragoons led by the Duke of Beaufort and all the leading gentlemen of the district. This was not simply an outburst of random and aimless violence by the miners. In the development of the disturbance and the behaviour of the crowd, there was evidence of order, discipline and purpose.

For twenty-one years past, about half the Forest had been locked up behind gates and fences which were designed to protect young plantations of oak and beech trees from grazing animals. Between 21 May and 8 June, anonymous night raiders destroyed some of these enclosures. Edward Machen, the Deputy Surveyor of the Forest, the chief resident Crown officer, and a magistrate offered a reward of fifty guineas for the discovery of the offenders but the only response came from an old miner who declared that he and his three sons had done the mischief and then laid claim to the reward.[13] It is not recorded that he was taken into custody. But this, however, was a minor problem, and only the prelude to a much more serious worry for Machen.

That became clear on 3 June. Warren James, a miner, had printed a notice which gave clear warning to the authorities that more damage would be done to the enclosures.[14] It read:

> Take Notice, that the Free Miners of the Forest, intend to Meet on Wednesday next for the purpose of Opening the Forest, and their Right of Common to the same, so long deprived and All those Persons who may chance to have Stock thereon contrary to the Rights and Privileges of the Miners; are here required to remove the same forthwith otherwise they will have their Stock impounded without Further Notice.

13 *Monmouthshire Merlin* 11 June 1831.
14 Depositions in the trial of Warren James, P20: Assizes 6/2.

He posted copies of this notice up "in the most conspicuous places; and that they might be more extensively circulated, a number were given to the attendants on a funeral from Whitecroft, which took place about that time".[15] Machen responded by appealing to James to drop the matter. "How can you think of misleading the people in this way? Machen asked him, "what are you doing?". He promised to read to anyone who came to see him the Act of Parliament which had ordered the construction of the enclosures.[16] No one accepted his offer. Machen then printed a counter-notice which contradicted James' assertion that the miners were entitled to open the enclosures. Only the Lords of the Treasury had the authority to do so, he warned, and without their sanction, such an act would be unlawful:

> and, therefore if three or more persons shall assemble for such purpose, all that are present will be guilty of a riot; and this Notice is given, that persons may not unwarily join such an unlawful assembly, and that the innocent may be safe and the guilty punished.[17]

Clear warning had been given on both sides. James was not apparently deterred by the invocation of the name of the Treasury Lords. He insisted that he was supported by an even greater authority. He variously asserted that he possessed, a charter or an Act of Parliament which set out clearly the 'rights and privileges' of the miners and gave the Forest over to them.[18] One of the rioters told the correspondent of the *Merlin* that James:

> through some nobleman in London … has discovered an old charter or act of parliament, giving certain rights to the Foresters of which they can never be deprived … that it was a document of undoubted authenticity, having been signed by seven English kings, amongst whom was his Majesty George the Fourth, who affixed his signature to it just before he died.[19]

And even more than that, James told his followers:

15 Ibid.
16 Ibid.
17 Depositions in the trial of Warren James, PRO: Assizes 6/2.
18 A Resident Forester, *The Life of Warren James, The Reputed Champion of The Forest of Dean, Descriptive of the Forest Riots, including an Account of John Harris Alias Poisefoot* (Monmouth: Heath, 1831) 19.
19 *Monmouthshire Merlin* 6 June 1831.

We have nothing to fear, for not only the King but the duke of Beaufort is on our side–he is the poor man's friend, and will see us righted.[20]

On the morning set for the miners' meeting, Machen approached James and demanded to know under what authority they would open the Forest. James indulged in no talk of charters or Kings but instead "with a face of the most imperturbable gravity produced as the voucher of his privilege, an enormous pick axe".[21] He then led the way to the Park Hill enclosure and with about eighty other miners began to break down its fences. Machen read the Riot Act but the mob ignored him.[22] Philip Ducarel, another of the Forest's magistrates, read the Act a second time twenty minutes later but that produced only laughter and jeers. Machen and Ducarel complained later that their presence seemed to make the rioters work with greater determination. What, after all, were the magistrates when the name of the King had been so confidently invoked? Moreover, they had only the inadequate force of a small band of unarmed woodwards[23] and special constables to support them.[24] The impotence of the authorities seemed to the foresters to confirm what James had said about the justice of the miners' cause and the great and powerful men who supported it:

> they are satisfied that the Crown agrees with them in opinion, because they gave formal notice of their intention to lay the Forest open some days ago; and contend that if the Government had been averse to their proceedings, they would have sent down military to stop them.[25]

The mob grew quickly. About 300 people joined it before the end of the first day. They included about eighty women who "seemed still more intent on the work of destruction than the men".[26] Over the next two days, messengers went from the mob to the Forest pits to bring those miners who were still at work to help pull down the fences.[27] The

20 The Life of Warren James, 27.
21 Monmouthshire Merlin 6 June 1831.
22 Depositions in the trial of Warren James, Evidence of John Longhorn, PRO: Assizes 6/2. 11. Magistrates to Home Office.
23 Woodwards are people who manage woodland.
24 Magistrates to Home Office, 11/0831, PRO: H052/12. Ds.
25 Gloucester Journal 11 June 1831.
26 The Life of Warren James, 21.
27 Monmouthshire Merlin 11 June 1831.

mob included, as well as Warren James and one or two others who may be identified as the working proprietors of small mines, workmen in larger mines, women and children and cottagers, that is, people who had land and a cottage in the Forest but did not work as miners.[28] One of them at least described himself as a "respectable farmer".[29] At its largest, the magistrates later reported to the Home Office, the mob numbered between two and three thousand people.[30] They remained in control of the Forest for four days and, using their time to good effect, levelling about sixty miles of fence. They breached most of the enclosures in some way and, in a number of places, drove cattle and swine in to graze on the undergrowth and acorns.[31]

Under the leadership of their captain, the rioters worked in an orderly and disciplined manner. As the miners came in from the surrounding pits, he divided them into parties of from fifty to three hundred which, accompanied by carts carrying provisions and cider, scattered through the Forest to the various enclosures where, under the direction of other leaders, they set to work on the fences "in the same way as they would have worked at anything else".[32] And hard work it must have been for them, not just the brief violence of a moment's anger. James' anonymous biographer wrote this description of the work:

> Their mode of proceeding was this; they took a few yards at a time, which a large body rushed on, and by mere muscular strength overthrew. This appears still more worthy of note, from the thickness of the walls, which were mostly composed of clayey earth, in some places seven or eight feet thick. Gorse of many years growth had strengthened these boundaries by shooting down roots into the earth of a prodigious size, and interlacing its branches in such a manner on the top, that it appeared to a spectator to require a work of time to effect its

28 No more precise account than this may be offered of the composition of the crowd. The reports of the riot in the newspapers used only such general terms as "workmen" or "cottagers". The reports in the newspapers of the Quarter Sessions and Assizes trials of some of the rioters do not identify the occupations of those tried. The depositions and other official papers of trials other than those for capital charges or treason have been destroyed. *Monmouthshire Merlin* 11 June 1831, *Gloucester Journal* 11 June 1831 and 20 August 1831; Beaufort to Home Office, 15 June 1831, PRO: H052/12.

29 *Gloucester Journal* 20 August 1831.

30 Beaufort to Home Office, 15 June 1831.

31 Ibid.

32 *Monmouthshire Merlin* 9 July 1831; Magistrates to Home Office (n.d.), PRO: HO 52/12; Depositions in the trial of Warren James, Evidence of James James.

overthrow and not that of two or three days. They first cut away some of the strongest of the roots and then proceeded in the way mentioned, tearing down all before them, and at the fall of each fresh piece giving loud and repeated cheers.[33]

In harmony with its discipline and good order, the mob made few threats of violence to people of private property. The rioters were "civil in their deportment but resolute in their purpose".[34] The magistrates wrote that "the mob offered no personal violence and indeed confined themselves wholly to the destruction of the fences". The only exception they noted was that on the Saturday night some of the mob went in straggling parties to beg for food and beer. They qualified this exception with the further note that "the farmers in general supplied them willingly".[35] The *Journal's* correspondent wrote similarly that the "rioters committed no other outrage, either in language or deed, than that of destroying the enclosures".[36] Pressing his point, he reported that when the magistrates left the enclosures after unsuccessfully reading the Riot Act on the first morning of the riot, "James sent for a constable, and in his presence superintended the work of destruction, observing that he had sent for him to keep the peace".[37]

This picture of a peaceful riot should be modified a little. One member of a party of rioters was very rude to John Langham, the assistant surveyor of the Forest. "It's through such b—-y rogues as you", he said, "that we have no more to eat, and I should like to cut your b—-y head off".[38] Another party threatened to put a woodward down a coal pit when they saw him taking down the names of the leaders, and offered to treat an unpopular bailiff in the same way if he appeared at the enclosures. A little later the mob levelled the fences around the house of a Mr Goold, the agent of the coal mine owner Edward Protheroe, and turned cattle in to graze in his garden. A threat to more substantial private property arose briefly when some in the crowd set up the cry to tear up the railroads. Nothing developed from that and the leaders were able to maintain the focus of the riot on the enclosures. These few incidents aside, there is nothing in the evidence to contradict the *Journal's* assessment that "altogether

33 *The Life of Warren James*, 22.
34 *Gloucester Journal* 11 June 1831.
35 Beaufort to Home Office 15 June 1831.
36 *Gloucester Journal* 11 June 1831.
37 *Monmouthshire Merlin* 11 June 1831.
38 *The Times* 15 August 1831.

they (the rioters) have behaved very temperately except in the act of destroying the enclosures".[39] The magistrates could do little to resist the mob, largely because:

> the feelings of the inhabitants, in general, are rather in favour of the proceedings of the mob and we have not been able to establish a constabulary force.[40]

Since a sufficiently large number of men would not come forward to help them, the magistrates despatched a message to bring soldiers. The first military intervention, however, only underlined the weakness of the magistrates and confirmed the miners in their opinion that the inadequacy of the government's response was evidence that their action had been correct. Since the regular troops in the Monmouth area were concentrated at Merthyr, where a much more serious disturbance was still in progress, only a makeshift group of soldiers composed of pensioners, militia and a marine recruiting party could be spared for the Forest.[41] Though armed, they did not impress the foresters who:

> having had intimation of their approach, hastened down to welcome them, and whilst they waited in the yard of the head inn, the "Angel", for orders, greeted them from without by the appellation of the "ragged regiment" and invited them up to the Forest, to see them at work.[42]

The Monmouth party marched out again the following morning after spending the night in a room above the Coleford market house, while the crowd cheered and jeered at them from outside.[43] The magistrates wrote later that they did not use this force to execute the warrants they had sworn for the ringleaders because they feared that they "could not without shedding much blood".[44] That was no doubt wise. Given the apparent contempt of the miners for the ragged regiment, it is unlikely that they would have submitted quietly. Again, the magistrates had appeared powerless and the foresters were jubilant. The departure of the troops:

39 *Gloucester Journal* 11 June 1831.
40 Magistrates to Home Office 11 June 1831.
41 Ibid.
42 *Life of Warren James* 7.
43 Ibid, and *Monmouthshire Mercury* 18 June 1831.
44 Magistrates to Home Office 11 June 1831.

was no sooner announced in the Forest, than the most enthusiastic joy was felt. They considered that they had now completely prevailed, and their rights were by this bold effort restored to them. They looked on themselves as masters, where they had long been servants.[45]

The miners' triumph was short-lived. They had the Saturday night to themselves but regular troops arrived on the Sunday. That event struck the *Merlin's* correspondent with awe:

The arrival in Coleford, on Sunday, of a squadron of the 3rd Dragoons, with their loaded pistols and carabines–their naked swords glittering in the sun–their limbs of Herculean mould– and their dashing military appearance, struck terror into the hearts of the bravest.[46]

A little after the advance guard, the rest of the Dragoons arrived in company with the Duke of Beaufort, the Marquis of Worcester, the High Sheriff of Gloucestershire, "every magistrate and gentleman of influence in the neighbourhood", and a party of special constables and woodwards.[47] This was a considerably more impressive force than Monmouth's ragged regiment and the rioters responded accordingly.

The advance guard had come at a trot with swords drawn, its colonel expecting to find the streets of Coleford running with blood, but the town was quiet.[48] There had been some reason to expect a more dramatic event since the rioters had declared from the beginning that they would meet force with force and would fight if soldiers were used against them. They declared it again at a meeting called on the Saturday night to consider the news that a regiment of horses was on its way to the Forest. They "all swore to stand to a man", but no one did.[49] One small party continued to work on the fences at Ruardean Hill after Beaufort's arrival, but when they heard that the Dragoons were riding towards them they too scattered to hide in the woods and coal pits.[50]

Authority, present now in full strength and with proper show, settled down to a selective and calculated punishment of the rioters.

45 *Life of Warren James*, 45.
46 *Monmouthshire Merlin* 18 June 1831.
47 Ibid.
48 *Life of Warren James*, 28.
49 Ibid, 27.
50 Magistrates to Home Office 15 June 1831.

The distribution of punishments reflected a distinction which the magistrates and press had made from the beginning between James and his followers. James, the leader, they saw as having a direct and personal responsibility for the riot.[51] The others were essentially good and loyal men who had been deluded by James and his talk of charters and rights. Most of the rioters consequently were not taken into custody. They were permitted to expiate their disloyalty by rebuilding the fences they had levelled, and this, at the last report of the matter, some of them were busily doing.[52]

Not all could be treated in that manner. It was necessary, the presiding judge said in his introductory remarks at the opening of the Gloucester Assizes to:

> satisfy all persons, that the law will protect those who are in peaceful enjoyment of property, and punish such as assemble riotously together, to the terror of his Majesty's subjects, to attempt to enforce their rights.[53]

To that end, seven men were indicted for causing riot and tumult. They were not charged as capital offenders, however, because "his Majesty's Attorney-General was of opinion that they had been acting under misguided notions". Found guilty, they received sentences ranging from one month to two years at hard labour with, for four of them, strong recommendations from the jury for mercy.[54]

Warren James could not be dealt with so leniently. The authorities believed it was his fault that the miners laboured under misguided notions and so he had to suffer the principal punishment. James did not disclaim his leadership of the riot once the Dragoons had arrived but, if his biographer is to be believed, played his part faithfully and with a full sense of its dramatic import right to the last.

The soldiers did not take him until the Wednesday following their arrival, when he was, in the correct manner, betrayed. At about midnight a party of foot soldiers concealed themselves around the pit in which James was hiding. William Watkins, one of the Keepers of the Forest, then gave the signal which James' sister used to "draw him to bank".

51 *Monmouthshire Merlin* 11 June 1831; *Gloucester Journal* 18 June 1831 and 25 June 1831; and see the warrant sworn for James arrest by Machen before the riot began. Depositions in the trial of Warren James, evidence of E. Machen.
52 *Monmouthshire Merlin* 18 June 1831 and *The Life of Warren James*, 37.
53 *Gloucester Journal* 13 August 1831.
54 *Gloucester Journal* 2 July 1831.

When James appeared in his pit dress, "almost as black as the coal he worked", the soldiers surrounded him. "I'm betrayed by treachery", he cried, "was not this the case, nine hundred men would have surrounded and defended me with the last drop of their blood! But do your duty; I have nothing to fear". Properly proud and defiant, he refused to change from his pit dress to appear before the magistrates: "No, I shan't; my dress is good enough for the company I am going in".[55]

At Gloucester, James was indicted with the capital offence of remaining with rioters for one hour after the reading of the Riot Act. The judge overruled his defence, that he did not remain with the rioters, on the grounds that no evidence was adduced to show that James actually did retire. The jury found him guilty but recommended mercy. Accordingly, the judge undertook to make as favourable a representation of the case to his Majesty as he possibly could and then recorded a judgement of death.[56] James made no statement about the riot, but said simply: "I don't care if they hang me, only let it lead to the good of my countrymen".[57] They did not hang him in the end but accorded him instead the dubious mercy of transportation for life.[58]

Here then was the miners' riot. The accounts of it which are left to us, apart from those contained in the letters which Beaufort and the magistrates sent to the Home Office, seem in places less concerned with accurate reporting of the affair than with creating a sense of drama–or melodrama–or displaying a condescending refusal to believe that the rioters knew what they were about. Still, it seems clear that the riot was not simply a spontaneous, casual outburst of violence. The miners, and the cottagers with them, had deliberately and in an orderly, disciplined manner, set themselves against the authorities in an assertion of their 'rights'. The event had been planned in advance and warning given to and received from the magistrates. The rioters were a 'mob' in the sense that they had ignored the reading of the Riot Act, but not in the sense that they were a disorderly rabble. What is not clear from this account so far, however, is the set of purposes and motives which impelled the miners to riot and tumult.

55 *Life of Warren James*, 35 – 36.
56 *The Times* 15 August 1831.
57 *Life of Warren James*, 44.
58 *Gloucester Journal* 20 August 1831.

Chapter Two

Motives

What purposes and motives lay behind the Dean miners' confrontation with the authorities? Leaving aside for the moment the problem of the enclosures, two obvious motives to seek in 1831 are the political and the economic. Was the Dean riot 'political' in the sense that it was part of the unrest and agitation which surrounded the promotion of the Reform Bill and the elections which followed the dissolution of Parliament at the end of April 1831? Was this riot of a kind with those at Bristol, Merthyr, Nottingham and Derby which Thompson has described as "insurrectionary climaxes to Radical agitation"?[59] Or was this riot a 'slump explosion': the product of distress, hunger and unemployment?[60]

This chapter will argue that, although there was political agitation among the miners, there is no convincing evidence that it was directly responsible for the riot. There is, however, some slight and unsatisfactory evidence that there was distress and unemployment in the Forest. This provides a first set of reasons for the miners' insistence on opening the enclosures. 'Distress' alone, however, helps little in understanding the riot. In expressing their demands and identifying the sources of their distress, the miners used the language of "ancient rights and privileges". They cast themselves as the victims of the State and of capitalists who had come into the Forest and deprived them of their customary rights. This suggests that the riot expressed a conflict between old ways of living and working and the new ways which the State and the capitalists had introduced to the Forest. This suggestion raises a number of problems which will be examined in the chapters which follow.

The demand for Reform was heard in the Forest as it was in the rest of England. A letter to the editor of the *Merlin* in January 1831, from 'Acornpatch', which described the foresters as "poor, poor, very poor", also described them ambiguously as "quiet, quiet and very quiet". He goes on to state that:

> we have not had a single instance of incendiarism, disloyalty, rebellion or riot, in any town, village, or hamlet between the rivers Severn and Wye, whilst our neighbours on every side have had repeated acts of diabolical pursuits.

59 Thompson, The *Making of the English Working Class*, 81.
60 E J Hobsbawm, *Industry and Empire* (London: Weidenfeld and Nicolson, 1968) 130.

Although there was great suffering in the Forest, he says that there was still:

> not to be found in any class (and I am in the habit of visiting all classes daily) an instance of strife-stirring persuasion; they generally and universally hold the unpardonable incendiarists in the greatest abhorrence.

This letter, with its emphasis on suffering, riot, and rebellion assumes the character of a warning, a word to the wise, in the light of a report on the following page of the *Merlin* that "an orator of the Cobbett school has lately been gulling the poor miners in the Forest of Dean by inflammatory speeches". A number of the miners collected together at Bream village to hear the orator "harangue them on some topics which they could not understand, and then obtained a number of signatures to different blank sheets of paper, which he represented as intended petitions for doing away with the truck system".[61] The clever orator moreover persuaded "many of the poor creatures" to subscribe money to promote his campaign. The foresters may have been quiet, quiet and very quiet, but at least one strife stirrer had been among them and at least some of them had signed his petition and given him money.[62]

Politics appeared more conspicuously in the Forest a month before the miners' riot, during the 1831 elections. The local Reform candidates, Sir Berkeley William Guise and the Hon. Henry Moreton, paid a visit to the village of Coleford on the edge of the Forest. A "great multitude of people" met them about two miles from the town with a band and flags on which were inscribed "Guise", "Moreton", and "Reform". The crowd took the horses from the carriages and drew them into the village amidst loud cheering. Speeches from the candidates on the subject of Reform were greeted with:

> Shouts of approbation from the Foresters, which our correspondent describes as the voice of so many roaring lions ...The blues (the anti-reformers) had a few windows broken; after which the multitude dispersed.[63]

61 Truck system or Tommy system is any arrangement under which wages are paid, partly or only, in the form of: payment in kind (i.e. commodities, including goods and/or services); credit with retailers; or a money substitute, such as scrip, chits, vouchers or tokens, rather than with conventional money.
62 *Monmouthshire Merlin* 1 January 1831.
63 *Monmouthshire Merlin* 14 May 1831.

A party canvassing for the Blue candidate, Lord Somerset, received a different sort of welcome. When "Lord Granville Somerset and several other gentlemen" came to Coleford about 500 pro-reform Greens followed them about and hissed at them. Since the population of Coleford in 1831 was 2,193 people, this was not an unimpressive turnout.[64] The Greens were:

> attended with a band of music, green boughs and flags, bearing inscriptions; a black flag was hoisted opposite the blue house, on which was inscribed 'Blues mourn for Somerset'. Lord Granville attempted to make a speech from the balcony in front of the Angel Inn, but the mob would not allow him to be heard. On leaving the town for Clearwell and Bream, the canvassing party was pelted with stones and boughs were thrust in their faces … Several windows were broken at the Red Lion, a house open for the Blues.

At the other Forest villages, Somerset's party met "a very indifferent reception".[65] It would be useful to know a good deal more about the election riot in Coleford, but unfortunately, there seems to be no evidence about it other than the newspaper report. Not even the limited evidence of voting figures is available because Somerset withdrew from the contest on the eve of the election.[66] The election riot, however, is probably a fair indicator that the Forest, though geographically isolated, was not cut off from the play of Reform and anti-Reform politics.

A fortnight after the Coleford election riot, and a fortnight before the miners' riot, a new political presence appeared in the Forest. A William Birt published the first edition of his unstamped newspaper, *The Forester*, on 26 May 1831.[67] Its principal content reflected two main purposes: firstly to demonstrate that the English social and political system was immoral and secondly, to argue that a number of problems peculiar to the Forest were a symptom of the oppressive working of the general system. The paper's motto, "All for Each and Each for All" epitomised Birt's demand for a society based not on the individual selfishnesses, which he identified as the source of poverty in England,

64 Population Abstracts 1831.
65 *Monmouthshire Merlin* 14 May 1831.
66 Ibid.
67 *The Forester* 26 May 1831.

but on a collective regard for the welfare and rights of all men: [68]

> The hostility generated by the fancied reality of individual advantage has been universally diffused, and men have employed their inventive energies to create means for the disadvantage and destruction of their fellow-creatures. But a bitter climacteric–an ultimate demonstration of the insanity of selfishness–is now beginning to dispel the doctrine which assumed that private interest and individual aggrandisement are compatible with general welfare. In the unnatural inequality of fortune, in the ferocious delights of despotism, in the constant efforts for increasing individual power is the effect of this doctrine discovered.[69]

English society, he argued, was dominated by the passions of sensual gratification and despicable avarice, and it worshipped at the shrine of sordid gain and bestial licentiousness. This immorality in society produced and was supported by the artificial and unnatural concentration of power and property in the hands of a few men who dispossessed the majority. [70]

Though profoundly corrupt England was not completely lost. A new political era had dawned and brought with it the chance of regeneration:

> the intensity of social evil has hastened the period of its decay. Extremes have arrived, and the balanced medium must be restored. There is an incipient but advancing perception, that the present perverted state is not unchangeable, that some analogy, between the advance of intelligence and the improvement of the social compact, must be gradually and extensively realised … The chains which bound mankind in darkness are rapidly corroding away, and the reign of despotism is verging to its close.[71]

England's hope was in general moral reform and, in particular, a Reform Bill from a Whig ministry. The paper was thus an advocate of Reform and a supporter of the green cause.

68 Ibid.
69 *The Forester* 2 June 1831 p 13.
70 *The Forester* 26 May 1831 p 3.
71 *The Forester* 2 June 1831, p 13.

But, as the Coleford election riot demonstrated, the voice of Reform had been heard in the Forest before. What was unprecedented in Birt's paper was that it alone, within the framework of Birt's general analysis, discussed problems peculiar to the Forest. While the Monmouth and Gloucester papers referred to the Forest only rarely, and then only to report specific incidents such as accidents and robberies, *The Forester* began with a discussion of the operation of the truck or 'tommy' system of wage payment in the Forest collieries, the use of waste land to help the poor, and the operation of the Forest mining and game laws. The discussion mirrored all the distinctions which Birt made in general terms between the rich oppressors, with all their artificial and unnatural power and the industrious majority. Birt aligned himself with "my poor fellow creatures, labourers in the Forest", against the "base and contemptible dastards" who operated the Tommy shops, "many of whom I knew to be steeped in poverty to the very lips, a few short years ago, who are now snorting and looking down upon your plain but honest wives and families with heartless contempt or filthy pride". "I say", Birt declaimed:

> that the hard working Forester ought to be treated like a man and an Englishman, by being paid his wages in money and left to his own choice in the disposal of it; 'Tommy' says he shall be treated like a Negro, and merely receive victuals for his work.[72]

This language was not likely to encourage loyalty and quiescence among the miners. Birt also questioned the government of the Forest. He described the laws which regulated mining and commoning in the Forest as a:

> chaos of mixed plunder, meanness, oppression and litigation, from which he can best extricate himself who has the amplest means of establishing might against right.[73]

It had not always been so:

> The good old straight-forward Foresters appear to have had a code of their own, which worked well and yielded a just apportionment of the Forest resources to the inhabitants at

72 *The Forester* 26 May 1831 p 8. NB the terms used are historically and culturally specific.
73 Ibid pp 7 – 8.

large, but now, from some cause or other, new laws and new results have the predominance.[74]

This contrast between the justice of the old laws and the oppression of the new he linked with, again, the contrast between the wealth of the few and the poverty of the many. The present laws produced on the one hand "pale and wan looking colliers" and on the other, men who:

appeared as frequently spruce, gay and waxing fat with the same temper as the ass emphatically alluded to of old. The Noblesse and Beggary of Italy in a petty way.[75]

Birt declared in favour of the Foresters, the real Foresters, "Those who work and toil for their bread".[76] Their condition had to be reformed. One way of doing that was to throw the Forest waste lands open to cultivation by the poor. Another was to remove the restrictions on the taking of game, whose effect was to tempt "the starving peasant" to crime and then to punish him for it with transportation to the charmless Antipodes. That system should not be tolerated in the reign of the Fourth William, "the King who has so wisely identified himself with the people".[77]

Here then, in the two weeks before the miners' riot, was a powerful new voice in the Forest: one which advocated Reform, took the part of the poor against the rich and questioned the government of the Forest. But how important was *The Forester*, how important was political agitation in general, in the making of the riot?

At the time of the riot, there were rumours of plot and conspiracy. The correspondent of *The Globe*, who referred to the rioters as "the levellers" and to the riot as "this levelling system", seemed to believe that the miners were the victims of the "seductive promises of wretches whose sole object is to make tools of them for their own purposes". He went on:

There is some movement in this business which demands prompt and strict investigation. The writer of this conversed with two men who were pressed on Thursday and compelled

74 Ibid p 73.
75 Ibid.
76 Ibid.
77 *The Forester* 2 June 1831 p 15.

to assist in throwing down the banks, and it is evident from their report, that the great majority of the foresters believe that Warren James, their openly avowed leader ... and who is the O'Connell of the Forest, is but the tool agent of some one or more noblemen in town who are determined to "see the foresters righted". It would not be prudent or just to use the names of the parties mentioned, for perhaps it is a licence taken by the leaders of the rioters without authority. A sister of James, it is said, lives with a nobleman, who the foresters expect will be in the forest shortly again, and James has been twice to town to have interviews on this business; one fact is evident, that the poor men are acting under the impression that they are committing no illegal act, and that no resistance will be offered them.[78]

Warren James' biographer accepted one version of the plot story. Sometime before the riot, he wrote, James' sister went to live in London and "from the acquaintance there formed, was led to believe the Foresters were a people denied their privileges and deprived of their birthrights". This she passed on to her brother who:

had long, though secretly, brooded over the desire of delivering himself and countrymen from what he felt and was persuaded was a thraldom ... his London friend, falsely so called, encouraged this desire; and Warren was firmly persuaded that he should find friends among the higher powers. Whatever form or name is possessed by the malign being who thus urged him on, it is a subject of regret that he cannot be held up to public odium so fully as he deserves.[79]

The first of these reports, however, was avowedly a rumour, and one couched in the vaguest terms. *The Gloucester Journal's* correspondent put the same rumour in a different light:

The most ridiculous reports are as usual current respecting the instigation of these riots. It is said that they are persons of wealth and rank and parliamentary influence, but such nonsense is scarcely worth repeating. The only known leader

78 *The Times* 14 June 1831.
79 *The Life of Warren James,* 14 and 15.

is the Warren James, whose name was affixed to the handbill inviting the Foresters to meet to lay open the Forest. [80]

The magistrates in their report to the Home Office equally disbelieved in a plot. Warren James, they reported, had gained great influence among the miners by:

> stating that he was countenanced by persons high in authority and by the Government itself … but we have no idea that (the miners) were assisted by any person of higher rank, or that the riots have connection with any political cause.[81]

There is nothing in the surviving Home Office or Treasury Solicitor's papers to suggest that the Government took seriously any suggestion that political agitation lay behind the riot. The Solicitor's lenient treatment of the rioters who were taken into custody, apart from James of course, suggests the contrary.

James' biographer was probably caught in an artistic trap of his own making. The purpose of the biography was to "consider the motives by which those misguided men (the rioters) were influenced".[82] His method was to draw a character sketch of the 'forester' which would make clear that, whatever else may have been true, the miners were not seditious men. Though rioters in other parts of the Kingdom, he argued, were looked upon with horror and detestation, the Dean miners were a special case:

> Whilst we view them with a disproving eye, as trampling on the laws of their country, the tear of commiseration will steal down the cheek of humanity, when pondering o'er the woes of a race of men so firm, so devoted — in a mistaken cause!

He went on:

> The Foresters were ever a distinct body of people; they lived on their own lands, were governed by their own laws, and stood firm for what they imagined their exclusive privileges. Bold, daring and truly hospitable … with spirits wild and free as

80 *The Gloucester Journal* 11 June 1831.
81 Beaufort to the Home Office, 15 June 1831.
82 *The Life of Warren James*, 3.

their native woods, hearts open and generous as their externals were rough and unpolished, they were at once the dread and veneration of their neighbours.[83]

Even the roughness of the forester was not as pronounced as it once had been. "In later years the spirit of the gospel which had been preached with evangelical purity" had exercised a benign influence on the miners, just as it had on the Esquimaux.[84] To this list of Virtues, he added, at the top, the ancient and selfless loyalty of the miners to their Kings. There was, however, a fatal flaw in the forester's character in that he had "a total ignorance of refined life":

It is related of one of them that being at an inn, and calling for a pint and a pipe, the servant brought them and also placed by his side a spittoon. John fidgeted for some time in his chair, and then gently removing it with his foot, expectorated on the floor. The girl, who prided herself on her housewifery, again placed the metal dish at his feet; John now lost all patience, he could command his temper no longer. "I tell thee what, wench", said he, "if thee doesn't move this cullender away, curse me but I'll spit in him".[85]

Thus the 'forester' was wild, brave, loyal and Christian, but not a little naive. And thus, the riot was not a terrible deed, but the pitiful act of a "misled, mistaken people".[86] All this, true of the foresters in general, was true of Warren James in particular. He was a man of considerable virtue:

From his youth, he was of a mild, reserved, and peaceable turn of mind, if anything, rather inclined to melancholy; he was what would, in refined society, have been denominated a sentimentalist. He was of the most abstemious habits and was often known to eat, after returning from church, on a Sunday morning, a dinner formed solely of vegetables, and repair thither again to attend the afternoon service. He disdained any show in apparel.[87]

83 Ibid, 4.
84 Ibid, 8.
85 Ibid, 8.
86 Ibid, 8–9.
87 Ibid, 12–13.

As might be expected, he was his widowed mother's favourite son and lived in her house until he was taken away by the soldiers. Even his part in the riot was indicative of virtue. He acted:

> not with the wild impulse of riot, but the calm determination of a man willing to resign private benefit for public good, as he has been frequently heard to say he would willingly give up his own life, if by that means he could gain his countrymen their liberties. He felt it a duty–he viewed it as an honour.[88]

How was it that this virtuous, selfless man could be the source of the delusion which misled the miners into riot? He could not have been seditious and disloyal because he was, after all, a forester. The insertion into the story of the shadowy, malign being in London avoids the contradiction leading to the conclusion that James was himself mistaken and misled. This is not to say that James had not taken advice in London. He had, in fact, consulted a solicitor there about the miners' rights and privileges. This matter will be discussed below in its proper context.[89] The point for the moment is that there is no reason to believe that there was any substance in the rumours of plot and conspiracy conducted by mysterious great men in London and certainly no reason to think the riot was the product of distant political manipulation.

What of William Birt and the *Forester*? Birt's catchphrase "King William and Reform" appeared once at the enclosures. It was written on a piece of paper handed to him by a rioter, according to Mr H. Davies, a banker from Monmouth who was present at the enclosures on the first day of the riot.[90] This, however, is the only reported reference to Reform on the event. If the riot was in some way promoted by Birt, more than might have been expected. It seems probable that the riot developed independently of him. The first night raids on the enclosures began on 21 May, before *The Forester* was first published, and, although Birt addressed himself to the problem of the poor and the use of the Forest for their relief, it was not until the issue dated 9 June 1831, the day after the riot had begun, that he took explicit notice of the threat to destroy the enclosures.[91] He was, moreover, in a very different position. Although his writing had been inflammatory, it

88 Ibid.
89 See below Chapter 5.
90 *The Times* 15 August 1831.
91 *The Forester* 9 June 1831.

had also been tendentious. If he wished to stir up the foresters it was to the end of Reform and the return of a Whig ministry. However, it was obvious before the riot that the cause of anti-Reform had fared badly in the general elections and that a Reform ministry would regain office.[92] That being so, Birt could not, without monstrous inconsistency, advocate anything resembling rebellion or a want of confidence in the enlightened leadership. His advice to the foresters, therefore, was to be calm and rational:

> I have heard that threats have been used to enforce the re-opening of the enclosures, these are very blameable, to give them effect would be decidedly illegal and wrong. The time now is, when just complaints will not only be received but redressed ... Never mind my good fellows, don't get waspish and angry with the flip-flaps and popinjays of things as they have been, just as they are about to die a natural death ... Try to get relief by every rational and constitutional means, but by no other ... Our old ship has been a long time on her beam ends, but we have got a good commander aboard and a capital pilot at the helm now, who ... will soon put her on sailing trim again, and bring her safe into port, where there will be, I hope, plenty of 'fresh provisions'. [93]

This was the theme of all Birt's subsequent comment on the affair, and none of it contributes to an impression that he was in some way directly responsible for the riot. On balance then it does not seem likely that the Dean riot was 'Political' in the sense that it was intended to promote the Reform Bill or that it was the result of direct political agitation. This is not to say, of course, that the general political context of the event was irrelevant. Explicit criticism of Government, the condition of the poor and the public statement of so many others of their grievances, may well have encouraged the foresters to attend to their own, to articulate them and to seek redress. The environment of political unrest and agitation, of Cobbites, Swingites and incendiaries, of attacks on the "popinjays of things as they have been", probably made the use of riot to draw attention to the miners' grievances seem a less extraordinary course of action than it might have in more settled times.

92 M Brook, *The Great Reform Act* (London: Hutchinson, 1973) Ch.6. The last returns from the general election of 1831 were in by June 1.
93 *The Forester* 9 June 1831 p21.

But it is unlikely that the Dean rioters were, for any political purpose, a hired hand "operating on behalf of external interests".[94]

If the riot was not the result of distant political manipulation or immediate political agitation, may it be regarded as the product of the economic recession of 1830–32?[95] The fragments of evidence about the Forest in this period which have survived do suggest that, like those in neighbouring Monmouthshire, the Dean miners were suffering distress in 1831.[96] In their report to the Home Office on the causes of the riot, the magistrates remarked that:

> the men in general have for the last 2 or 3 years suffered considerable privations for want of full work, having many of them not more than 2 or 3 days work in a week. This has caused dissatisfaction.[97]

The *Gloucester Journal's* correspondent also drew attention to the economic background to the riot. "The real cause of the evil", he wrote, "is a want of labour and of sufficient wages, so as to enable a man to live, and procure for himself and family the necessaries of life".[98] In March 1832, a meeting of free miners at Yorkley in the Forest made much the same point. The meeting resolved that:

> a large portion of the Working Class of this Forest, together with their numerous Families, are great Sufferers for Want of Employment; to which cause they ascribe entirely the recent Disturbances which took place in the Forest.[99]

A letter to the *Merlin* in January 1831 described the "labouring classes" in the Forest as suffering "great and severe privations from the general distress", and another report in the same edition referred to the

---

94 Rude, *The Crowd in the French Revolution*, 239.
95 See D E Aldcroft and P Pearson (eds.), *British Economic Fluctuations 1790 -1939* (1972); P Deane and W A Cole, *British Economic Growth, 1688–1959* (New York: Cambridge University Press, 1962); and A D Gayer, W W Rostow and A J Schwartz, *The Growth and Fluctuation of the British Economy* 2 volumes (Oxford: Clarendon, 1953).
96 *Monmouthshire Merlin*, 12 March 1831 and 5 March 1831. See the debate between coal owners and proprietors of the Monmouth Canal. Though they were in dispute about other matters they agreed that "the depression in the iron and coal trades is almost insupportable, and that as an unavoidable consequence the operative classes are brought into a state of comparative suffering".
97 Beaufort to the Home Office, 15 June 1831.
98 *The Gloucester Journal* 11 June 1831.
99 Resolutions of a meeting of the Free Miners and Colliers of the Forest of Dean, 5 March 1831.

miners' "present distress".[100] Later, on 2 June, *The Forester* reported that Bilson colliery had closed and "a great number of men once employed in this colliery are now standing still because the people interested in the tonnage dues will not submit to an abatement thereof".[101] Bilson's owner, Edward Protheroe, asserted that a reduction of tonnage dues was necessary because the Forest's coal was too dear to compete with cheap coal from Monmouth, Shropshire and Staffordshire".[102]

Another symptom of distress in the Forest, and one which links it more directly to the riot and the breaking down of the enclosures, was *The Forester's* brief campaign for the opening of the Forest's waste lands to the poor in the two weeks before the riot. The paper derided charity as a means of aiding the poor in a system, based on the rule of property, which offered the labourer "at best nothing but labour and pinching want and too frequently places him below the condition of the brute that perisheth".[103] Charity would make the labouring classes beggars in their circumstances and beggars in spirit. Would "it not be better to remove their necessity, by affording to the poor the means of maintaining themselves in their own right?" In the cause of "humanity, justice and sound policy", the paper advocated opening the Forest's eight thousand acres of waste land for cultivation by the poor.[104]

The edition of 9 June 1831, the Thursday of the week of the riot, contained an open letter "To the King", which informed His Majesty of "great loyalty and great poverty" in the Forest, "where great and general distress pervades a large body of industrious men, their wives and children". The letter asked that the industrious but suffering labourer be allowed to cultivate the "various and extensive tracts of land in the Forest of Dean, now wholly useless and unprofitable". Allowing it:

> would meet the claims of humanity, by affording him (the labourer) honourable and English-like relief, take away from the middle classes an onerous and unjust Burthen, quiet the feelings and apprehensions of the upper grades, and add stability, Power, and dignity to the nation at large.[105]

100 *Monmouthshire Merlin*, 1 January 1831.
101 *The Forester* 2 June 1831, p 15.
102 *The Forester* 28 July 1831, p 15.
103 *The Forester* 26 May 1831, p 6.
104 Ibid.
105 *The Forester* 9 June 1831, p20.

The Foresters' rhetoric, of course, was designed for the purposes discussed above. Nonetheless, its printing of the two items, their reference to distress in the Forest and discussion of a possible solution, confirm the impression, which the other few surviving fragments of evidence create, that the riot took place in the immediate context of distress among the Dean miners and their families.

This provides a first set of reasons for the riot by the miners and other cottagers. They were hungry. To help relieve their distress they wanted the use of the otherwise useless waste land in the Forest for gardening and the pasturing of animals and fowls. They had made application to the Commissioners of Woods for Permission to do this but had been refused. They, therefore, took direct action:

> The miners say that when Lord Lowther was the Chief Commissioner, the Foresters had applied to him for the throwing open of the Forest, and he was disposed to listen to their application: that the Duke of Wellington had appointed to meet him in the Forest for the purpose of inspecting the state and condition of the trees. The death of the late King, and the consequent dissolution of the Parliament, and breaking up of the Wellington Administration, prevented any further proceeding. It is said that since that time the Foresters have memorialized the present Commissioners of Woods and Forests on the subject but without success … Under the persuasion that they have been unfairly dealt with … they have taken the work of their real or supposed grievances into their own hands.[106]

The matter, however, was more complicated than that. The miners attributed their distress not only to the enclosures of eleven thousand acres of the Forest but also to:

> the influx of foreigners of whom they are very jealous; they have for some time been holding meetings for the re-establishment of their (Mine Law) Courts, but it has been stated as the opinion of the highest Law authorities that they would not be revived without an Act of Parliament. It is difficult to explain why a dissatisfaction on this ground should lead to the attack on the

106 *Gloucester Journal* 20 August 1831.

Forest Inclosures but this was certainly the most prominent ground of complaint.[107]

By the term "foreigner" they meant any person who had been born beyond the borders of the Hundred of St Briavels.[108] In this context, the foreigners were capitalists who had acquired control of part of the mining industry in Dean and who had built railroads there. The rioters asserted that they would drive them from the Forest and tear up the railroads.[109] In justification of this, they declared that they were attempting to reclaim "our rights and nothing but our rights".[110] The press, the magistrates, and the Government, all so far as it is possible to tell, believed that the "war word, as usual, is a restitution of rights".[111] Though none of them agreed that the miners had any or that, in any case, they ought to assert them by rioting. These rights were not those of the free-born Englishman but those of the free-born miner. These rights were encoded in the ancient code of customs and privileges, and the Mine Law Court that enforced it, which had once governed mining in Dean but was now largely inoperative because the miners complained, the foreigners and the Crown together had destroyed it.[112] Was this riot then of a kind with those eighteenth-century disturbances which, Thompson wrote, favoured:

> social conservatism. They are generally most evident when resisting change, defending established rights or customs or conditions; and the characteristic ideology is in the appeal to precedent. Legitimation is sought in appeal to Statute or ancient right: for food rioters, the legislation against forestalling, or even the old Book of Orders: for Spitalfields weavers or Lancashire weavers to wage assessment: for framework knitters to the Charter of the Company: for shearmen to the Act of Charles the second.[113]

Was the Dean riot a demand for the maintenance or restoration of a traditional way of working in the face of "capitalist innovation"? [114]

107 Beaufort to the Home Office, 15 June 1831.
108 Ibid.
109 *Gloucester Journal* 20 August 1831.
110 Ibid.
111 Ibid 11 June 1831.
112 *The Forester* 4 August 1831, pp 81-82.
113 Thompson, *The English Trade Unionism*, 21.
114 Rude, *The Crowd in History*, 226.

But the analysis is raising more questions at this point than it is answering. Who were the 'free miners' and what were their ancient rights and privileges? Who were the foreigners and how had they interfered with the free miners? What had been the relationship between the Crown and the foreigners, and the Crown and the free miners? Different answers to these questions will sustain different interpretations of the riot. It is the purpose of the chapters which follow, therefore, to provide answers sufficient to allow detailed insight into the situation of the three main groups involved as participants in, or objects of, the riot.

Chapter Three

The Old System in the Forest

The Forest of Dean in the eighteenth century was a rich but unprotected economic resource. Beneath the soil there lay a coal basin surrounded by deposits of limestone, iron ore and 'grindstone'. Above the ground, there were oak and other trees, whose wood and bark were of value to dockyards, coopers, tanners and farmers. There was stone, suitable for use in building, and there were deer, apples and herbs. All this belonged to the Crown which farmed the trees to provide timber for the Naval Dockyards.

At some time in the obscure past, the Crown had granted the right to take the coal and ore to a group of men who styled themselves 'free miners'. They worked under the watchful eye of the Mine Law Court which regulated the industry according to the ancient customs of the free miners and jealously guarded it against intrusion by foreigners. The miners' pits were small and, by and large, worked by the men who owned them. However, the miners and their families did not depend solely on the coal for their livelihoods. Under the lax system of Forest administration of the eighteenth century, they were able to turn the other resources to their own account. Miners encroached on the Forest by building cottages and enclosing land for gardens and orchards, pastured animals in the woods and stole the timber, bark and herbs. There were probably inequalities among the miners, both in the amount of land they held and the extent to which they participated in the ownership of the mines. Overall, however, the dominant pattern was that of mixed family economies based on small scale, independent proprietorship of land and mines and the harvesting of the Forest. The principal feature of the old system in the Forest stands out as it offered economic opportunity even to relatively poor men.

Two separate hierarchies of officials administered the nation's Royal Forests. The first was concerned with the Forest's primary purpose and value for the Crown, as a supplier of timber to the Navy, began with the Treasury in London. They appointed a Surveyor General of Woods and Forests who had as his assistant a Deputy Surveyor who was in control of each particular Forest.

In the Forest of Dean, the Deputy Surveyor overlooked the work of the Keepers of the six 'Walks' into which the Forest was divided for administrative purposes. Sharing local authority with the Deputy

Surveyor and the Keepers, were six verderers who were responsible for preserving 'vert and venison'.[115] They tried and punished such offences against Forest Law as poaching. A number of other offices, such as that of King's bowbearer, had only ceremonial purpose by the eighteenth century.

A nobleman headed the other hierarchy of control as Constable of the Castle of St Briavels and Lord Protector of the Forest. He was the King's man, responsible for mediating between him and his subjects in the Forest on all matters other than those concerning the timber. Through the Gavellers and Deputy Gavellers and the Mine Law Court, he supervised the mining industry and saw that the King had his share of profit from it. He also conducted a court which adjudicated claims of debt among the foresters and maintained a debtor's prison at the Castle. The Marquis of Worcester, the Duke of Beaufort and the Earl of Berkeley acted as Constables from time to time during the eighteenth and early nineteenth centuries.[116]

The Deputy Surveyor was the principal resident officer. He was responsible for guarding and managing the timber and ensuring an efficient supply of it to the Naval Dockyards. He received orders from them for quantities of timber, marked out the necessary trees and supervised their felling. From time to time he also held public auctions of timber and wood to obtain revenue for administrative expenses. He was also responsible for making and maintaining enclosures for protecting new growth.

While the Navy's demands constantly depleted the stock of trees in the Royal Forest, the supply of timber from private sources contracted as woodland was enclosed and turned to other uses. Since an oak took about one hundred years to mature, advance planning and planting were necessary to ensure the future supply. For that purpose, and to protect the young growth against grazing animals, an Act of Charles II had provided that the Crown might enclose and remove from all other uses 11,000 acres of Dean Forest, about half its area.[117] At the beginning of the eighteenth century, these enclosures were probably in good order and the Forest efficiently managed as a timber nursery.

---

115 Venison refers to the deer and vert refers to all that bears green leaves in the Forest.
116 The Third Report of the Commissioners appointed to enquire into the State and Condition of the Woods. Forests and Land. Revenues of the Crown and to sell or alienate Fee Farm and Unimproveable Rents, 1788, pp.26-27. This report will be referred to from here on as L.R.C., 1788.
117 The Dean Forest (Re-afforestation) Act, 1668. 20 Chas II c.3.

While the Crown reserved the farming of the timber to itself, it allowed the coal to be mined by a specially privileged class of men who styled themselves 'free miners'. The free miners' 'rights' are obscure in origin, but were probably settled in their main outlines by the end of the thirteenth century.[118] The first formal statements of them which are extant date from the seventeenth century; the first printed copy from 1687. The "Laws and Customs Of the Miners in the Forrest of Dean", as the book was entitled, was the result of an Inquisition by forty-eight free miners at some time before 1610, at which they co-ordinated and wrote down all that was remembered about the customary rights.[119] This was what the miners called their "Book of Dennis", and this, new editions of which were printed in 1800 and 1830, was probably the ancient document from which Warren James drew his authority.[120] The Book expounded:

what the Customs and ffranchises hath been that were granted tyme out of minde and after in tyme of the Excellent and Redoubted Prince King Edward unto ye miners of the fforreste of Deane and the Castle of St Briavels and the bounds of the said fforreste.

It asserted the miners' right to take coal and ore from:

every soyle of the King's of which it may be named and alsoe of all other folke without withsaying of any man.[121]

As well, they might build roads for the carriage of coal from the mine to the nearest King's highway and might take timber from the Forest for use in the pits, without cost.[122] In return, the miners were to pay a royalty on production to the King through the Gaveller, who

---

118 See C E Hart, *The Free Miners of the Forest of Dean*, (Gloucester: British Publishing Company, 1953) Chapter 2.
119 The Laws and Customs of the Miners in the Forest of Dean, in the County of Gloucester, in *The Compleat Miner*, issued by W. Cooper "at the Pellican in Little Britain" (1688). A copy is held in the Gloucestershire Collection of the Gloucester Public Library (Ref. No. 16655) with an earlier manuscript copy of the Laws and Customs. C E Hart has reprinted in its entirety in his *Free Miners*, and annotated, a 1673 transcript of the laws. Clause numbers given here correspond to Hart's paragraph numbers. Further references here will be to L.& C., followed by the relevant clause number
120 Nicholls, *Iron Making in the Olden Times*, 65 and see Hart, *The Free Miners of the Forest of Dean*.
121 L. & C., Clause 12.
122 Ibid, Clauses 13 and 26 – 28.

was also to be responsible for registering the mines and seeing that the customary modes of working were enforced.[123] If the Lord of the soil was someone other than the King he too had a right to a royalty or share in the mine. In more detail, the Book also prescribed the distances to be kept between pits, the size of containers to be used in carrying the coal, and the procedures to be followed when workings met underground.[124] The Book also pronounced on three matters that were to be in dispute in the nineteenth century. It stated that:

> Alsoe every miner in his last days and at all times may bequeath and give his dole (share) of the mine to whom he will as his own cattle. And if he do not the dole shall descend to his heirs.[125]

Did this mean the miners had the right to sell "to whom he will"? This clause was at least ambiguous and was later interpreted by some free miners to mean that they might sell a coal holding to a foreigner. Clause 30 of the Book seemed to exclude foreigners from the mines:

> Alsoe no stranger of what degree so ever he be but only that been born and abiding within the Castle of St Briavels and the bounds of the forest as is aforesaid shall come within the mine to see and know ye privities of our sou'aigne Lord the King in his said mine.[126]

Again, there was some ambiguity in this. Certainly, foreigners were excluded by Clause 30 from entering the mines and, therefore from working in them and becoming free miners. It does not, however, specifically prohibit foreigners from participating in the industry as non-working partners. On the third matter which later came into dispute, the Book was unambiguous. All disputes among the miners were to be tried before the Mine Law Court, presided over by the Constable, the Castle Clerk and the Deputy Gavellers. Matters were to be judged, with no foreigners present, by juries of twelve, twenty-four or forty-eight free miners whose decisions were to be final and binding. The miners might not plead in any other court on any issue touching the mines. As well,

123 Ibid, Clauses 15–19.
124 Ibid, Clauses 31, 34 and 40.
125 Ibid, Clause 24.
126 Ibid, Clause 30.

the Court might make further laws and regulations for the government of the industry.[127]

The Mine Law Court operated in the seventeenth and eighteenth centuries as a sort of trade association, governing the industry on behalf of the "Society of Free Miners".[128] The Court operated in the manner set out by the Book of Dennis. Matters were decided by juries of free miners whose jurisdiction was final and exclusive. Miners were encouraged to hold to the Court and to enforce its decisions by a regulation which awarded to the plaintiff half of any fine imposed on a man he successfully sued for breach of custom.[129] Occasionally the Court established the size of the measures to be used in selling and carrying the coal and set and varied the prices to be charged to different customers in different places. To ensure that the miners set their prices in accordance with the scale, the Court sometimes appointed panels of 'Bargainers' whose job was to arrange prices with regional or industrial groups of customers.[130] To defend its regulations and jurisdiction, the Court from time to time declared and collected quarterly levies on all miners and coal carriers to provide funds for legal expenses.[131]

The Court's primary function was to limit entry to the industry. Unlike those in other 'free mining' districts, as Dobb has pointed out, the Dean miners set up restrictions against newcomers.[132] Only the sons of free miners who had been born in the Hundred of St Briavels and who had served, to their fathers or other free miners, an apprenticeship of a year and a day were permitted to become free miners.[133] The sons of fathers not born free had to serve an apprenticeship of seven years if they wished to gain their freedom.[134] The only exception allowed to these rules was that the Court might create honorary free miners who were entitled to the usual franchises and privileges.[135] The Court further guarded against the intrusion of outsiders and the concentration of economic power in the hands of a few men, by stipulating that only free

127 Ibid, Clauses 20–23.
128 Forest of Dean, Deputy Surveyor's Office, Records, PRO F.16. See also Hart, *The Free Miners*, Chapter 4, in which he reprints entirely the surviving records of the proceedings of the Court. References to the Orders which follow will cite the Order number and its date. Order No. 16, 2/3/1741.
129 Order 9/3/1675 and Order No. 16, 2/3/1741
130 Order No. 16, 2/3/1741.
131 Order No. 3, 9/3/1675, Order No. 8/12/1685, Order No.10, 27/1/1701, Order No. 11, 1/7/1707 and Order No.15, 6/12/1737.
132 M Dobb, *Studies in the Development of Capitalism* (Rev. ed. 1949), 243 – 244.
133 Order No. 1, 18/3/1668.
134 Order No, 15, 6/12/1737.
135 Order No. 17, 22/10/1754.

miners should carry the coal to market and that no carrier should have more than four horses for his business.[136] There was no ambiguity about the Mine Law Court's intention to closely limit the industry to native miners and to exclude foreigners.

The Court, however, ceased to function, probably in 1775, for reasons which are not at all clear. No contemporary evidence survives to suggest why the Court went out of existence. Fifty-three years later, however, Thomas Davis, a free miner aged eighty, said in evidence before the Dean Forest Commissioners, who were inquiring into the miners' rights, that:

The Mine Law Court was given up, because of a dispute between free miners and foreigners, whom we did not consider fit to carry on the works. I believe the Court was given up because somebody took all the papers away from the Speech-house, and they were considered to be stolen. The Gaveller, one John Robinson, was a partner in the Fire Engine and was supposed on that account to have taken them away.[137]

A memorial to the Commissioners from Mr Clarke on behalf of the Free Miners made much the same point, though it did not name Robinson specifically:

That the foreigners finding the Mine Law Courts an insuperable obstacle to their success and more particularly by the orders last quoted of 1775, there was no chance of their being permitted to work in the mines, found that the only means by which they could hope for success was to destroy the Mine Law Courts. That the documents of this court were always kept in the Speech House in the Forest of Dean, but that after the conclusion of the last court in 1775, some person or persons broke open the chest in which they were contained and removed them.[138]

These accounts are not implausible. The last meeting of the Court had reaffirmed the prohibition against foreigners:

136 Order No. 5, 19/9/1682 and. Order No. 15, 6/12/1737.
137 The Fourth Report of the Dean Forest Commissioners, 1835, Appendix No. 1, p.17, The Reports of the Dean Forest Commissioners will be referred to from here on as D.F.C. followed by the number of the report.
138 Ibid, p 51.

Clause 16: Foreigners having any mine or coal work carried on in the Hundred of St Briavels, shall sell it to some free miner by private contract if they can, or otherwise expose it to sale by auction, by the Mine Law Court.

Clause 17: If a free miner dies and leaves his mine or coal works by will or testament to a foreigner, or it comes to him by heirship or marriage, he shall sell it as aforesaid, or hire free miners to work for him.

Clause 18: If any free miner sells any mine or coal work to a foreigner, he shall be liable to a penalty of £20, to be recovered in the Mine Law Court.[139]

That there was a need for this restatement suggests that there was some tension between miners and foreigners. Who were the foreigners? Some of the officers, Deputy Constables and Deputy Gavellers, had been made honorary free miners at one time or another, probably for services rendered the miners. And some of the honorary men had opened three mines: the Oiling Gin or Fire Engine, the Brown's Green and Gentlemen Colliers. In each case, they had taken foreigners into partnership with them.[140] This, it seems likely, produced the resolutions of 1775. Two of the partners in the Fire Engine were John and Phillip Robinson, father and son, and both Deputy Gavellers. One of them was also Clerk to the Mine Law Court and had possession of the records.[141] The inference which all this suggests is that John Robinson had stolen the records and then, in his capacity as Deputy Gaveller, had refused to hold the Court again because there were no records. The records reappeared in 1832: in the hands of Phillip Robinson, son and grandson of John and Phillip and assistant to the Deputy Gaveller.[142]

None of this is ultimately convincing, but Thomas Davis' account is at least plausible. But whoever took away the records, the cessation of the Court had no important immediate consequences. The three mines in which foreigners had a share were a small minority of the total number of mines, and one of them at least, the Fire Engine, later passed back into the hands of free miners.[143]

139 Ibid, p 44.
140 Ibid, p 7.
141 Ibid, pp 32-33.
142 Ibid.
143 Ibid, p 7.

These cases, involving the Forest officers, were the only substantial intrusion by foreigners before about 1800. This was probably so because of a successful defence of the custom by the miners in 1752. The Governor and Company of Copper Mines in England had enclosed land for their own mining and had attempted to exclude the free miners from it. William Collins, aged 77, deposed in 1832 that "'the miners tried to stop the company and could only do it by cutting under and letting the company's work fall in."[144] In other words, the mine was destroyed by free miners tunnelling underneath it and causing its collapse. The Company sued a party of miners for damages in the Court of the King's Bench but their action failed when the jury found in favour of the miners who pleaded the customary right to mine wherever they wished.[145] Any large scale, systematic attempt by foreigners to open mines in the Forest was thus vulnerable to undermining, against which they had no remedy at law.

The industry which worked within the framework of the custom was made up of relatively shallow pits and levels which worked the outcrop of the seams in the Forest coal basin and were limited in extent by the difficulty of dealing with water in the coal. The coalfield was roughly contiguous with the borders of the Forest. It was a synclinal basin of fourteen seams which outcropped in three rough concentric circles, broken in places by faults: the lower measures marched with the ridge of hills which circumscribed the Forest; the middle measures outcropped in the narrow valley which separated the outer ridge from the central plateau, and the upper measures made up part of the central plateau.[146] Where they could the miners took advantage of the slope of the seams to help with drainage. Nicholls wrote this description of the workings:

The existing remains of the coal-works of this period, combined with the traditions of the oldest surviving colliers, enable us to form an accurate idea of the way in which the workings were carried on. 'Levels' or slightly ascending passages, driven into the hillsides till they struck the coal seam, appear to have been general. This was no doubt owing to the facility with which they effected the getting of coal where it tended upwards into the higher lands forming the edge of the Forest Coal Basin, since

144 Ibid, p 33.
145 Ibid, p 7.
146 See F M Trotter, *The Geology of the Forest of Dean Coal and Iron-ore Field* (London: HMSO, 1942), Chapters 5 and 7.

they required no winding apparatus, and provided a discharge for the water which drained from the coal beds. The usages observed at this time at the works entitled the proprietors of their respective levels to so much of the corresponding seam of coal as they could drain, extending right and left to the limits awarded by the gaveller … If the vein of coal proposed to be worked did not admit of being reached by a level, then a pit was sunk to it, although rarely to a greater depth than 25 yards, the water being raised in buckets, or by a water wheel engine, or else by a drain having its outlet in some distant but lower spot … the chief difficulty being found in keeping the workings free from water, which in wet seasons not infrequently gained the mastery and drowned the men out.[147]

Steam engines might have been able to overcome the problem, but the capital necessary for their installation was probably not available in the Forest. The foreigners who might have supplied the capital were in general excluded by the custom. By 1788, only the one steam engine or 'fire engine' had been set up in Dean.

The miners conducted the works in 'companies'. Until 1824, when David Mushet published his survey of the strata, knowledge of the outcrop depended on local experience.[148] Though any miner might sink a pit wherever he chose it was a matter of chance and judgement whether he would strike coal. Sinking a pit was thus to some extent a speculative venture. The miners spread the risk and achieved a necessary concentration of capital and labour by forming 'companies' into which each 'vern' or partner had an agreed 'dole' or share of the profit. One of them, the 'first man in the fellowship', acted as leader of the company:

the strict custom required that the mines should be worked by companies of four persons, called verns or partners, the King considered as a fifth … all the verns were required to be free miners and to proceed in driving and working the level, or sinking and working the water pit, by their own labour, or assisted by their sons, or by apprentices.[149]

147 Nicholls, *The Forest of Dean*, 238–239.
148 Trotter, *The Geology of the Forest of Dean,* 21.
149 D.F.C., 4, p 8.

Under this system, the ownership of the mines was spread among a fairly large number of men and was not concentrated in the hands of a few. There are two estimates of the number of mines and miners in Dean Forest, for 1787 and 1798 respectively. The first comes from the report of the Surveyors William and Abraham Driver to the Commissioners of Woods and Forests in 1787.[150] According to them, there were ninety-eight mines at work in Dean in 1787, controlled by sixty-six companies of miners. It is not possible to tell how many miners made up each company. (See Table 1.)

In 1788, however, the Keepers were asked to report the numbers of miners in their Walks.[151] Four returned answers which included the numbers of men, women and boys working; one did not distinguish between men and boys; and one provided no information at all, except the number of miners. These figures are shown in Table 2. The four Walks which provided complete data contained seventy-one mines and 229 miners, an average of 3.22 per mine. So, it appears that the old custom of having four verns to a mine had broken down. The averages ranged from 1.86 men per mine in Speech House Walk to 5.5 in Littledean Walk. There were 106 mines in the Forest altogether, which, at an average of 3.22 men per mine, employed about 341 men.

On the same basis, the total number of people working in the mines was 473 including 341 men, 6 women and 126 boys 'working their freedom'. This is a fairly crude estimate but the obvious scope for error is not such as to invalidate an overall conclusion that small scale, co-operative proprietorship characterised the industry at this time.

Ownership was, however, not evenly distributed. Though about two-thirds of the companies held only one mine, the other third had multiple holdings. Twelve companies had two mines each, five had three, one had five and another seven. There is no means of assessing the significance of this distribution of ownership since no record survives of the size of each mine. Some of the multiple holdings may have comprised several pits or levels in the one "gale" or mineral holding. There is a strong hint of gradation and inequality among the miners in a report from the Gaveller that some of them were "so poor that no money can be collected from them, and there are great arrears of compositions (royalties) due".[152] There is, however, nothing to suggest the inequalities

150 Abraham and William Driver, *Particulars of a Survey of the Forest of Dean in the County of Gloucester* 1787. PRO: F.16/31.
151 L. R. C., 1788, Appendix No. 25.
152 Ibid, Appendix No, 25.

Table 1: Ownership of the Forest of Dean mines in 1787.

Number of mines controlled by each company	Number of companies	Total number of mines
1	47	47
2	12	24
3	5	15
4	-	-
5	1	5
6	-	-
7	1	7
	66	98

Source: Abraham and William Driver, Particulars of a Survey of the Forest of Dean in the County of Gloucester, PRO, F16: 31

Table 2: Workers in Forest of Dean mines in 1788

Walk	Mines	Free miners	Ave. miners per mine	Boys	Miners and boys	Women	Total	Ave. workers per mine
Speech House	7	13	1.86	8	21	2	23	3.28
Worcester	17	81	4.77	17	96		98	5.76
Littledean	8	44	5.5	27	71		71	8.87
Parkend	39	91	2.33	22	113		113	2.89
Subtotals a	71	229	3.22	74	303	2	305	4.29
Ruardean	28	-	-	-	133	4	137	4.89
Subtotals b	99	-	-	-	436	6	442	4.46
Blakeney	7	-	-	-	-	-	-	-
Totals	106	341.32*	-	-	-	-	472.76**	-

* 341.32 is the total number of mines times the average number of miners in Subtotal a.
** 472.76 is the total number of mines times the average number of workers in Subtotal b.
Source: L.R.C., 1788, Appendix No. 24, Examination of the Keepers.

which would be evident only forty years later when Edward Protheroe alone owned thirty pits and employed between 400 and 500 men.[153]

The miners were not the only inhabitants of the Forest, though they were probably the largest single group. There were as well "about twenty-two poor men, who at times when they had no other work to do, employed themselves in searching for and getting iron ore in the old holes and pits in the said Forest, which have been worked over many years".[154] About forty others worked at stone quarrying and another eighteen at lime-burning.[155]

Some other men were probably employed at the quarries and kilns and as woodsmen for the Keepers, but there is no record of how many there were. The other industries which had long been established in Dean, such as iron and charcoal making, tended to be located in small villages in the parishes surrounding the Forest.[156]

The miners, the other foresters and the Crown officials, under the lax system of management of the eighteenth century, created a situation in which:

> the encroachments there are more numerous, the perquisite and undue advantages taken by the officers more exorbitant and destructive, and the waste and depredation more rapid than in any other forest belonging to the Crown.[157]

What the Commissioners of 1788 saw as "waste and depredation", were, of course, for others, a source of income, a means of providing food and housing and of adding in diverse ways to a mixed family economy. The accounts which are left of the spoil of the Forest in the eighteenth century provide a glimpse of a way of life in which families were not solely dependent on wage labour for their livelihoods and were probably able to achieve something of the independence of peasant proprietorship of land.

According to the Commissioners, the waste in the Forest followed from an Act of Parliament in 1701 which restricted the right of the Crown to alienate its land, by sale or gift. Gentlemen of substance and property had once paid close attention to the Crown Lands and

153 See below Chapter 4.
154 L.R.C., 1788, Appendix No. 25.
155 A.& W Driver, *Particulars of a Survey of the Forest of Dean in the County of Gloucester.*
156 See C E Hart, *The Industrial History of Dean* (Newton Abbot, David and Charles, 1971).
157 L.R.C., 1788, p.562.

Forests because they were potential sources of grants and revenues to themselves as rewards for services to the Crown. The timber and the mineral deposits of Dean Forest had several times been granted away to individuals in that manner. But since that was no longer possible after 1701, the attention of gentlemen of rank and Ministers of the Crown lapsed.[158]

Those who held the ancient offices of Verderers, Foresters and Woodwards lost interest in the Forests and allowed to fall into disuse the courts which they were bound to maintain to enforce the Forest Law. The books of the Surveyor General of Crown Lands which dealt extensively with the Forest of Dean in the seventeenth century contained only a few references to it in the eighteenth. Checks on the Surveyor General and his Deputy and the resident officers were inoperative. No books were kept and no system of thoroughly regulating the felling of timber maintained.[159] The Forest lay open to daily abuses and depredations. The Conservator of Dean Forest, Mr Christopher Bond, complained to the Treasury in 1736 that:

After the Act 20 Charles II, 11,000 acres had been enclosed. The officers were duly elected, forest courts held and offenders prosecuted and punished, by which means were raised a great quantity of timber trees, but within the last 30 years these elections had been neglected, the courts discontinued, and offenders left unpunished, the officers of Inheritance, and others were grown remiss and negligent; so that a few enclosures, and those of a few acres only of the said 11,000 acres, were kept up, and these not carefully repaired; a great number of cottages were erected upon the borders of the forest, the inhabitants whereof lived by rapine and theft; there were besides many other offences committed such as intercommoning of foreigners, surcharges of commoners, trespasses in the Fence Month and Winter Haining[160] and in the enclosures; keeping hogs, sheep, goats and geese, being uncommonable animals in the Forest; cutting and burning the nether vert, furze and

158 Ibid, pp.21-22. The Act was the Civil List Act, 1 Anne c.5.
159 Ibid, pp.21-26.
160 Every year the authorities cleared the commoners' animals from the Forest during the Fence Month and the Winter Heyning. The historical reasoning behind the Winter Heyning was to keep commoners' animals off crown land in the winter so they would not compete for food with the King's deer when food was in short supply. The Fence Month was around midsummer and animals were kept off to avoid disturbing the fawning of deer.

fern; gathering and taking away crabs (apples), acorns, and mast; and other purprestures[161] and offences; carrying away such timber trees as were covertly cut down in the night time; by which practices several hundreds of fine oaks were yearly destroyed, and the growth of others prevented. It is feared that some of the inferior officers of the Forest, finding the offenders to go on with impunity, were not only grown negligent, but also connived at, if not partook in, the spoil daily committed.[162]

Fifty years later the assistant to the Deputy Surveyor in Dean made a similar retort to the Commissioners of Woods and forests:

The number of cottages and encroachments in the Forest he believes is nearly doubled since he has known it. The persons who inhabit the cottages are chiefly poor labouring people, who are induced to seek habitations in the Forest for the advantages of living rent free and having the benefit of pasturage for a cow or a few sheep, and of keeping pigs in the woods. The cattle of all the cottagers are impounded when the Forest is driven by the Keepers, as all other cattle are; and when the owners take them from the pound (paying the usual fees to the Keepers) they turn them again into the Forest, having no other means of maintaining them. The greater numbers of the cottagers are from the neighbouring parishes; but there are also a great many from Wales, and from various parts of England remote from the Forest: they are detrimental to the Forest, by cutting wood for fuel, and for building huts, and making fences to the patches which they inclose from the Forest; by keeping pigs, sheep, etc. in the Forest all year and by stealing timber.[163]

This situation resulted in part from the system of remuneration of the Forest officers. The Deputy Surveyor and the Keepers were paid partly by salary and partly through a scale of perquisites which must once have been so designed as to encourage the officers under adequate supervision, to attend properly to their duties. In other words, a sort of payment by results.[164] (see table 3)

161 Wrongful encroachment upon another's property such as woodland.
162 Ibid, p.23.
163 Ibid, Appendix No.39.
164 A perquisite is an incidental payment, benefit, privilege, or advantage over and above regular income, salary, or wages.

Table 3: Perquisites of the forest officers.

A. The Deputy Surveyor in the Dean Forest.
1. The tops of all Naval timber refused by the Purveyor of the Navy as unfit for Naval use.
2. The tops of all stolen timber.
3. All trees felled by wood stealers.
4. One moiety of the cordwood made from the offal wood of timber delivered to the miners and of stolen timber.*
5. In some Walks of the Forest 4d and in others 6d for every tree felled for the use of the miners.

B. The Keepers.
1. On Deer
   a. On every warrant for killing a buck: £1. 1s
   b. On every warrant for killing a doe: £10. 6s
2. On the Herbage
   For trespassing on the Forest in the fence month and winter heyning:
   horses, mares and horned cattle: 4d each
   colts, unshod: 1s each
   sheep: 2d each
   hogs, ringed: 4d each hog
   hogs unringed: 1s each
3. On Timber and Wood
   a. On every order for delivery of timber to the miners: 1s.
   b. Moiety of all offal wood, of timber cut for the miners.
   c. Moiety of all cordwood of stolen timber.
   d. All lengths or pieces of stolen timber (called kibbles).
   e. The bark of timber delivered to the miners.
   f. A portion of fines imposed on timber stealers.

* Cordwood is logs cut to a length of about 4 feet to facilitate stacking and generally used for fuel or making charcoal.
Source: L.R.C. 1788, Appendix No. 24, Examination of the Keepers.

Consider, by way of example, the division of an oak tree felled by timber stealers. If the Keeper found it before it had been carried off, he was entitled to a share of the offal wood and all the bark of the tree. The body went to the Deputy Surveyor. If the stealers had cut the tree into cordwood or kibbles, the Keeper had a share of them. Similarly, the Keepers received one shilling for every order of timber for the miners and a share of the offal wood and the bark of miners' timber. These perquisites, together with a reward to the Keeper for every timber stealer convicted, encouraged the officers to look out for timber stealers and to regulate closely the supply of trees to the miners.

Table 4: Returns from office to the keepers 1788 (amounts in £s).

Walk	Keepers salary	Annual value of land and lodge	Value of perquisites	Total return from office	Non-salary income as % of total
Speech House	22	40	208	270	91.85
Blakeney	22	33	78	133	83.45
Worcester	22	30	73	125	82.40
Littledean	22	30	78	130	83.08
Parkend	22	30	98	130	85.33
Ruardean	22	24	113	159	86.16

Source: LRC, 1788, Appendix No. 24, Examination of the Keepers.

A fee for each animal taken into the Pound when the Keepers drove the Forest at the winter heyning and the fence month encouraged them to protect the young growth from grazing animals. But, obviously enough, without adequate supervision and bookkeeping, these same perquisites encouraged the officers to connive at the very offences they were meant to prevent. The more timber stolen, the more delivered to the miners and the greater the number of animals allowed to roam in the Forest, the greater the return to the Keepers in the way of perquisites and fines.[165]

Some idea of the extent to which the officers benefitted from the exploitation of the Forest is given by the returns of income they provided to the Commissioners of 1788.[166] (See Table 4). The basic salary paid to the Keepers was only £22 per annum; with perquisites, they admitted to incomes ranging from £95 to £230, excluding the value of their lodges and land. They had each enclosed, either for pasture, crops or orchards, between 21 and 40 acres of the Forest the value of which, together with that of their lodges, brought their total estimated returns from office to between £125 and £270 per annum. On top of that, they each kept substantial numbers of stock: horses, cattle, sheep and pigs. (See Table 5). The Deputy Surveyor in Dean admitted to a total annual return from office of between £300 and £500, of which £50 only was salary.

The Forest officers, however, were only one term in the equation of exploitation. The inhabitants were another. At the beginning of

165 Ibid, pp.28-30.
166 Ibid, Appendix No. 26.

Table 5: Keepers land and stock.

Walk	Land enclosed (Acres)	Stock
Speech House	49	4 horses, 4 colts, 4 Bullocks, 6 pigs, 40 sheep
Blakeney	30	20 horses, 6 oxen, "a few pigs", 80–100 sheep
Worcester	30	3 horses, 2 bullocks, 2 pigs, 30 sheep
Littledean	30	3 horses, 5 cows, 6 cattle, 3 pigs, 60 sheep
Parkend	30	2 horses, 4 cows, 6 cattle, 3 pigs, 60 sheep
Ruardean	28	I horse, 4 oxen, 6 pigs, 8 geese

Source: LRC, 1788, Appendix No. 24, Examination of the Keepers.

the eighteenth century, there had been no inhabitants since, after the Act 20 Charles II, the Keepers had cleared the Forest of cottages and cabins.[167] By 1788, however, with the relaxation of control, some 1,433 encroachments had been made, taking in about 1,350 acres of land: an average of 0.3.35 acres (acres; roods; perches) per encroachment. (See Table 6).

It is difficult to tell how much land was held by each encroacher because, although the survey which provides the data lists the names of encroachers, it does not show the consolidated total holding for each person. Where a name appears more than once in the lists it is not possible to tell whether one man had a number of holdings or whether several men sharing the same name had separate patches. Only where separate patches lay beside one another is it possible to tell that they belonged to the same person. However, the upper and lower limits to individual consolidated holdings may be established by consolidating first those patches which lay beside one another and clearly belonged to the one person and, secondly, by consolidating all patches held in the same name.

The former procedure produces a total of 1,165 holdings of an average size of 1.0.30 acres (acres.rods.perches); the second, 899 holdings and an average size of 1.2.70 acres. Of the 899 holdings, about half were of less than one acre and about 95% were of less than five acres. At the other end of the range, seven people or less than one % of the total

167 Ibid, p.20.

Table 6: Encroachments in the Forest of Dean in 1787.

Total forest area (acres.roods.perches)	24,714.2.29
Encroached area (a.r.p.)	1,385.3.21
Patches of land enclosed (No.)	1,433
Average size of patch (a.r.p.)	0.0.35
Patches which lie beside one another, are listed together and belong to the one encroacher (No.)	1,165
Average size of adjacent patches (a.r.p)	1.0.30
Patches held in the same name (No.)	899
Average size of patches held in the same name (a.r.p.)	1.2.7

Source: Abraham and William Driver, Particulars of a Survey of the Forest of Dean in the County of Gloucester, P.R.O., F 16:31.

had enclosed more than ten but less than fifteen acres of land. The 899 holdings shared 593 cottages, mostly made of stone, but also of wood, turf, mud and rush. Over 90 % of the 899 owned one cottage or none. (see Table 7). About eight % or 73 people had two, three or four cottages. At the upper possible limit of concentration of land and cottages, then, most foresters had only one cottage and less than five acres of land. A small group, perhaps 13 people, had either two or three cottages and between five and fifteen acres of land. This conclusion must be qualified in that the larger holdings shown in the table may have been the result of combining those of two or more people with the same name.

Another important qualification should be made. The table does not allow for family group working of land. Several times the Surveyor uses the terms "senior" and "junior" to distinguish in his list between father and son of the same name. Where one or the other is not shown as having a cottage it would probably be fair to assume that the two patches should be treated as a family holding. One group name does appear in the lists to suggest the possibility of family co-operation: Joseph Mountjoy and sons had 3.2.7 acres of land in eight separate patches.

Moreover, about 45% of the 899 encroachers of the table had no cottage. The 96 cottages which were part of multiple holdings probably account for, say, one-quarter of them. The balance may have lived in the villages surrounding the Forest. But given the obvious advantages

Table 7: Encroached land times number of cottages in Forest of Dean 1787.

No. cottages held by each encroacher	Area of land held by each encroacher (acres)					Totals	%
	0–1/2	1/2–1	1–5	5–10	10–15		
0	174	79	138	13	1	405	45.05
1	130	85	189	12	5	421	46.83
2	1	8	36	6	-	51	5.67
3	-	1	13	6	1	21	2.34
4	-	-	1	-	-	1	0.11
Totals	305	173	377	37	7	899	
%	33.93	19.24	41.94	4.12	0.77		100

Source: Abraham and William Driver, Particulars of a Survey of the Forest of Dean in the County of Gloucester, P.R.O., F 16:31.

of living on extra-parochial land and being close to the pits, the timber, and the encroachment, this seems unlikely. It is more probable that more than one member of a family living in one cottage had made encroachments. However, even on the generous, though arbitrary assumption that all those who had no cottage were contributing to a family economy the 494 'family' holdings which remain average only 2.3.12 acres each.

Cultivation on this scale did not make the foresters entirely self-sufficient. Corn, in particular, they obtained from the farmers in the surrounding countryside in exchange for coal. When the Government bought up large amounts of corn for the army in 1795, the resulting scarcity created a disturbance among the miners. They rioted and seized grain from wagons and barges that were carrying it from the country. The riot was suppressed by soldiers and two men were hanged. To alleviate distress the Government distributed £1,000 worth of grain among the foresters. This incident suggests that the miners were vulnerable to shortages of grain and fluctuations in its price, despite their smallholdings.[168]

As well as building cottages and enclosing land for gardens and orchards, the foresters pre-empted to their own use the areas which

168 Nicholls, *The Forest of Dean*, 84-86.

had been reserved for nurseries under the Act 20 Charles II. They kept animals and turned them loose in the woods to graze. So that the animals might have better pasture, the foresters burnt off the undergrowth:

> The colliers most of them have houses on the verge of the Forest, and in order to procure grass for their horses, often set fire to the grass or furze, and by that means the bushes are destroyed … there are many acres of the Forest from that cause now wholly destitute of trees, which was formerly covered with timber. They also take in part of the Forest for garden ground and keep a great number of hogs to run in the Forest … there are many acres, in different parts of the Forest so broken up by the hogs, that the ground appears as if it had been ploughed and harrowed or rather like a summer fallow.[169]

Enclosures, of course, interfered with the pasture, so the foresters simply tore down the fences and carried them off for sale in Bristol.[170] Consequently, where there had been 11,000 acres of enclosed land at the turn of the century, there were only a few acres in 1788.[171]

Then, of course, there was the opportunity, or temptation to turn all that fine timber to their own account. Timber stealing was an important problem in the eyes of some at least of the officers who had to do with the Forest. The Purveyor to the Navy in Dean wrote to the Treasury in 1770 that:

> he had discovered and was informed of the most shameful depredations of the oak timber, which was cut every day by persons living around the Forest; and that for some years it had been the custom to steal the body of the tree in the night, and cut it into coopers' ware, leaving the top part on the spot which the keepers take as their perquisite; and that at that time whole trees were conveyed every spring tide to Bristol; and that when he was at Gatcomb, in one day there were 5 or 6 teams came with timber planks and knees winter felled, and other timber

169 Mining Claims and Disputes; details of encroachments, depredations and abuses in the Forest. Representation to The Treasury, from the Office of Woods, Appendix 5. PRO: F.20/2. Referred to from here on as Mining Claims and Disputes.
170 L.R.C., Appendix, No, 39.
171 Ibid, pp 22-23.

among which were several useful pieces for ships of 64 and 50 guns.[172]

He proposed that rewards be offered for the capture of offenders, but rewards proved to be of little use for two reasons. The first was that even if men were apprehended it was difficult to convict them because of:

> the lenity of the Magistrate before whom some of the offenders have been carried, and the unwillingness of the juries, by whom others have been tried, to give a casting verdict (even on satisfactory proofs being adduced) against persons guilty of stealing only the King's timber, a practice many of the persons residing in or near the Forest, appear to have been so long habituated to as to render it in their eyes only a trifling misdemeanour, if an offence at all.[173]

Even if a conviction were recorded the magistrates left profit to the stealers:

> Some little time back, Bennett, the Keeper, detected a man who had peeled off the bark of fine oak trees standing in Worcester walk; the offender was fined five pounds: this, although considered a large fine, was certainly inadequate to that offence; as exclusive of having destroyed the growth of the trees, the bark stolen and carried away was of more value than the fine imposed.[174]

On balance, the thing was still worthwhile. And, what if the man could have both the profit and the reward for his own capture? A system of rewards introduced in 1791 had to be discontinued because:

> advantages are said to have been afterwards taken, by Confederates in the depredation, of the largeness of the reward and the mitigation of the penalties inflicted, to divert to their own emolument what had been meant to secure their punishment thus fully defeating the object in view.[175]

172 Ibid, Appendix No.37. Report of the Solicitor of the Treasury, relative to Depredations committed in Dean Forest
173 Mining Claims and Disputes, p 1.
174 Ibid, p51.
175 Ibid, p64.

The miners' right to take timber for their works provided the opportunity for more timber stealing. The Deputy Surveyor complained to the Commissioners in 1788 that:

> the great waste, spoil and destruction of the timber and wood on the Forest is and hath been occasioned by an improper application of the timber delivered to the miners for the use of their works, he … believes that one moiety or one half part of the timber which they have had delivered to them would have been more than sufficient to have answered every needful purpose to which it ought to have been appropriated … he hath frequently seized large quantities of offal timber, and much other timber as the miners could not use in their works (in 1783) he seized and took 586 feet of oak timber, and more than 200 pieces of cleft oak on the grounds of one George Martin … he also seized, at the Fire Engine on the Forest, between two and three wagon loads of timber, hewn up and converted by the colliers into coopers' ware for market.[176]

Earlier in 1780, the Navy Office reported stealing by the miners to the Treasury and commented that it is well known, they now live more by timber stealing than by any other business.[177] The Surveyor General, asked about the report, replied dolefully that "the complaints are but too well founded".[178] There is no way of telling how much timber was stolen or what it returned to the stealers and miners, far less the contribution timber stealing made to family earnings. But some reports suggest strongly that this was not an insignificant activity. It was sufficiently important for the Forest officers to employ men at their own expense to cut timber for the miners. For example, Thomas Harvey whose son is a dealer in bark and timber and was the Keeper of Speech House Walk:

> had six men constantly employed in felling and stripping miners' timber during the last spring and summer, as long as the bark would run … that practice had been continued with the knowledge and connivance of the Deputy Surveyor, as long as any profit could be made by the stripping of the bark.[179]

176 L.R.C., 1788, Appendix No. 23.
177 Mining Claims and Disputes, p287.
178 Ibid, p 288.
179 Commissioners of Woods to Treasury, 29/4/1789, PRO: Crest40/62.

The same Deputy Surveyor who was so forthright in attributing waste and spoil to the miners was himself a man whose considerable enterprise suggests something of the importance of timber stealing to the Forest's economy:

> In our third Report to Parliament, we took notice that the Deputy Surveyor in this Forest had a contract with the Navy Board, for supplying a certain quantity of timber to the Dockyards, as a timber merchant on his own account, and mentioned among other things facts acknowledged by him, his having employed agents to buy for his own use, the greatest part of the timber sold by himself as Deputy Surveyor, under a warrant issued in 1786 for raising £2,000 towards building Gloucester gaol. This same officer is also a considerable dealer in bark and exports large quantities of it to Ireland in vessels of his own, built in his own dockyards at Lydney, within a few miles of the Forest. [180]

On a lesser scale, women and children could add to the family income by harvesting bark and fern. Timothy Mountjoy's account of this part of the life of a Forest of Dean collier probably refers to the early nineteenth century but may also be taken as an indicator of the ways in which families could use the Forest in the late eighteenth century:

> I have heard my mother boast of the money she used to get at bark scraping, that was to follow the men who stripped the bark off the oak trees. The bits of bark not so big as a man's hand or finger were picked up and sold at a fabulous price to what it is now; I believe it was 3/6 or 7/6 a cwt.; there were many who all the summer followed bark scraping. There was another thing women were employed in, that was to go day after day into the woods to cut, and then to burn, the green fern, to make ley to put into the hard water to wash our clothes and the clothes of the aristocracy. After we burnt it we gathered it up in baskets and damped it with water, and made it up in baskets into balls about the same of an orange, and sold them by the dozens to the shops in Gloucester ... Another thing many of the Forest women got good wages at, and many of

180 Ibid.

the men, was birch stripping. As soon as the birch came out in leaf then the season began; we went into those parts of the Forest where it was plentiful, each one cutting a stick just as your hand would clip round the top, hit it into the ground, slit it at the top, and begin the day's work. My mother and two of my sisters would strip off the rind almost as fast as I could cut it, because it wanted cutting to a certain length, then bleach it in the sun, take it home, tie it up into bundles with two bands round them like a besom, only so small then take them to the clothing factories and sell them at 2/6 a dozen, if they were of good quality. Mother would trot off in a morning with eight dozen on her head, and return by ten at night.[181]

The use of the Forest in all these ways, for mining, cottages, gardens and timber stealing, all followed, from one form or another of co-operation among the Crown, its officials, the miners and the other inhabitants. One symptom of this was the creation by the Mine Law Court of honorary free miners: some fifty-one of them between 1700 and 1754.[182] Some of them were Deputy Constables but many also the lesser officials, the resident Forest officers, including the Deputy Gavellers and Deputy Surveyors. There was as well, however, occasional conflict among them:

Whereas a notorious and villainous gang of persons have several times of late assembled themselves together in a riotous manner and committed diverse disorders by breaking open the pounds at the Castle of St Briavels and Park End Lodge, and discharged from thence several cattle. And upon Saturday night, the 5th instant, the same gang came to the Lodge of Mr R. Worgan, entered his garden, beat down his beans, cut up his cabbages and apple trees, broke his windows, and part of the pound wall; then adjourned to the Speech House Lodge which is in the possession of George James, commonly called Captain Whithorne.[183] Upon their coming they immediately fell to work on the Pound, but being desired by the Captain to desist who rose to the window to disperse themselves, they returned him for answer a brace of slugs in at the window. The

181 Timothy Mountjoy, *Sixty Two Years in the Life of a Forest of Dean Collier* (1887) 76.
182 Hart, *The Free Miners*, 142-144.
183 *Gloucester Journal* 22 July 1735.

Captain upon that ply 'd them warmly with small shot, who sent him in return a great Quantity of slugs and balls, so that almost a continual fire lasted for nearly half an hour, when their ammunition being spent, they had something else to pick besides stones out of the pound wall. On the morrow, one of the gang was taken and on Monday committed by Thomas Pyrke Esq. to Gloucester Castle; but his company being apprised of it, seven of them disguised themselves in a dreadful manner, and armed with four guns and three swords, came several miles over the Forest but finding their comrade gone too long before, returned back to pull off their two ragged petticoats and clean off their too much like Devil's faces. But it is to be hoped the gentlemen of the county will lend an assisting hand to put a stop to these desperate and resolute fellows. N.B. They are supposed to be what are called Fanside men and come from in or about Clowerwell.

Forest officers blamed the tendency of the miners to violence for the prevalence of timber stealing. The Surveyor General reported to the Treasury in 1780 that:

the offenders were become so daring and desperate, as to bid defiance to his deputies and render every attempt of his, in a summary way, totally ineffectual; in the preceding month, a number of persons in disguise had openly cut down two large timber trees at Yorkeley in Dean Forest and wounded several keepers who attempted to oppose them.[184]

The miners' right to take timber could not be summarily curtailed because "they are too numerous and formidable a body to be wantonly refused". [185] Mr Blunt, the Deputy Surveyor, also wrote that if the miners "took it into their heads to fancy that they had a legal right to oak timber, they would use none other, and that, if not delivered to them, he had not a doubt, but they would take it by force". [186] These reports, though they should be heavily discounted in the light of the obvious self-interest of the officers who made them, do perhaps indicate that relations between the foresters and the authorities were governed in part

184 L.R.C., 1788, Appendix No, 37.
185 Mining Claims and Disputes, p291.
186 Ibid, p 319.

by the threat of force. But violence between the officials and the foresters was conspicuous mostly through its absence. There is no suggestion that they were in competition for the spoil of the Forest. Why should they have been? The old scale of officers' perquisites provided a useful guide to the division of the spoil and one which had the sanction of settled usage.

Here then, in summary, is a glimpse of what the Forest offered to the miners in the eighteenth century. The account given here is incomplete and unsatisfactory in a number of important ways. There is no way, for example, of telling precisely how many miners and other foresters there were or how the returns from the mining industry and the spoil of the Forest were divided among them. That, and other gaps in the evidence, make it possible to offer only tentative sorts of conclusions. None the less, it is possible to see in the matrix formed by the richness of the Forest's resources, the laxity of the administration, and the venality of those who were meant to administer it, the outlines of varied, and not inconsiderable, economic opportunity for those who lived there.

The miners could have, and only they could have, the coal under the soil. Until 1775 at least, they sheltered behind the Mine Law Court and the customs and privileges of the 'free miners'. The Court, operating as a "closed corporation, with collective regulations and collective functions",[187] excluded outsiders from the industry and, by enforcing the customs, enforced a basic equality of opportunity to search for coal among those who were free miners. By regulating the carrying trade it guarded against the intrusion of middlemen and the concentration of economic power in the hands of a few.

The decision in the Copper Company's action for damages against a party of miners probably acted as a barrier against foreigners after the collapse of the Court. The Court could not, of course, stipulate equality of luck and skill. Some mines were undoubtedly worth more than others and some free miners better off than others. The problems posed by wet coal seams, and lack of capital, probably, however, prevented the development of very great inequalities in the size and worth of the mines.

The Forest provided cottages, fuel, gardens, orchards and pastures for animals. Timber and the herbage provided income for the men who worked in gangs to steal it or take it, ostensibly for use in the mines, as well as employment and income for women and children in the bark season. In contrast with the Forest officials, the miners encroached

187 Dobb, *Studies in the Development of Capitalism*, 244.

on the Forest on a small scale. Most had only one cottage at most two or three acres of ground, a scale of cultivation which perhaps did not maintain the foresters at much above subsistence level and could not supply such essentials as grain. There were no rates or taxes to pay, no schools or schoolmasters, no churches or ministers, no soldiers or constables or large-scale employers.

Only the Crown officials represented authority, and could restrict the miners' ability to exploit the Forest as they chose–and the officials had an interest in not restricting them. This, however, rough and inadequate it is, is a sketch of a community of small proprietors and land holders who had a considerable degree of freedom from authority and of opportunity to contribute to the family economy in diverse ways. Their independence, and their holdings in mines and land, sprang, on the one hand, from the laxity of the Crown administration of the Forest and, on the other, from a set of laws and customs which gave the free miner his individual and collective identity, distinguished him from those other men who were not 'free', and defined his 'rights' against those of all other men.

Chapter Four

Forest Reform and the Foreigners

By 1831 the old system in the Forest had all but disappeared. Foreigners had control of the largest part of the mining industry and the Crown had reasserted its administrative control. Where they had been independent proprietors, the free miners had become, in general, wage labourers and their use of the Forest had been severely curtailed. How had this come about? More particularly, given the later complaints by the miners, had the Crown and the foreigners acted as allies in despoiling the free miner of his rights? What part did the free miners play in the development of the new system?

This chapter will argue that the Crown had at first resisted the intrusion of the foreigners and had been well aware of the likely consequences of an invasion of capital. Expediency, however, and the interests of the Crown, demanded an alliance with the foreigners against the free miner. But the alliance of Crown and capital was not alone responsible for change. Some free miners welcomed the new order and attempted to turn it to their own advantage. Some co-operated with the foreigners and allowed them to acquire title to the coal through fraudulent use of the miners' ancient privileges.

Perhaps the most important source of change in the Forest was a new sense of the 'public interest' in central administration. The seventeen Reports of the Commissioners of Woods and Forests followed on those of the Commissioners of Public Accounts which had enunciated the principles of 'economical reform' in the Civil Service. That philosophy, among other things, asserted the primacy of the demands of the State and the public over those of office holders under the Crown:

> We do not mean to violate, in the slightest degree, any right vested in an officer by virtue of his office. The principles which secure the rights of private property are sacred, and to be preserved inviolate; they are landmarks to be considered as immovable. But the public have their rights also, rights equally sacred, and as fully to be exercised … The principle which gives existence to, and governs every public office, is the benefit of the State. Government requires that various branches of business should be transacted, and persons must be found to transact them. The acceptance of the public office implies an

engagement to do the business, and a right to compensation. The officer had powers delegated to him necessary for the execution, but he has no other right than to the reward of his labour.[188]

Behind the reports of the Commissioners of Woods, there lay the same concern for the public interest and the benefit of the State, in the light of which they measured the adequacy of the administration of the Forests and the Crown officials' performance of their duties. As Chapter three indicated, the Commissioners found the officials in Dean wanting in their attention to duty and remiss in not protecting the rights of the State. They recommended accordingly, among other things, that yet more Commissioners be appointed to inquire into and rectify the problems of timber stealing and the miners' use of timber, to set encroachments on some correct legal basis, to revise felling regulations and to alter the system of payment of Forest officers.[189]

Little was done about these recommendations until in 1803, Lord Glenbervie took office as Surveyor-General of Woods.[190] By then the demands of the Navy in war had given the problem of timber supply some urgency. Nelson himself visited the Forest in 1803 and reported:

The Forest of Dean contains about 23,000 acres of the finest land in the kingdom, which I am informed if in a high state of cultivation of oak, would produce about 9,200 loads of timber fit for building ships of the line every year; that is, the Forest would grow in full vigour 920,000 oak trees. The state of the Forest at this moment is deplorable, for if my information is true, there is not 3,500 loads of timber in the whole Forest fit for building, and none coming forward ... where good timber is felled, nothing is planted, and nothing can grow self sown: for the deer (of which now only a few remain) bark all the young trees. Vast droves of hogs are allowed to go into the woods in the autumn, and if any fortunate acorn escapes their search, and takes root, then flocks of sheep are allowed to go into the Forest and they bite off the tender shoot ... Trees cut down in swampy places, as the carriage is done by contract,

188 *The Eleventh Report of the Commissioners to examine, take and state the Public Accounts of the Kingdom*, 1783 printed in part in H Roseveare, *The Treasury 1680 – 1780* (1973) pp.149-150.
189 L.R.C., 1788, p41.
190 *The Thirtieth Report of the Commissioners of Woods* (1852) p223.

are left to rot, and are cut up by people in the neighbourhood
… There is also another cause of the failure of the timber: a set
of people called Forest Free Miners, who consider themselves
as having a right to dig for coal in any part they please; these
people, in many places, inclose pieces of ground, which is daily
increasing by the inattention, to call it by no worse name, of
the Surveyors, Verderers etc who have the charge of the Forest
…. knowing the abuses, it is for the serious consideration of
every lover of his country how they can either be done away
or at least lessened … If the Forest of Dean is to be preserved
as a useful forest for the country, strong measures must be
pursued.[191]

Glenbervie agreed with him. "The two principal objects in the
administration of this, as well as the other Royal Forests," he wrote,
"ought to be":

(1) To preserve from depredation and waste, and to turn to the
utmost practicable account the wood growing there.

(2) To adopt such measures, and act upon them steadily and
without discontinuance, as shall render the Forest productive
of as great a successive quantity of Navy timber particularly,
and of any other wood not interfering therewith, as shall be
compatible with their extent, the nature of the ground, and the
rights belonging to the individuals therein.[192]

Accordingly, he deprived the Forest officers of their land and
perquisites and subjected timber felling to book-keeping and inspection.[193]
In 1806, by means of a new Act of Parliament, he reasserted the terms of
the Act 20 Charles II and directed that 11,000 acres of Dean be enclosed
and planted.[194] This task Glenbervie gave out to private contractors who
finished it in 1818.[195] Encroaching and timber stealing were gradually

191 *The Thirtieth Report of the Commissioners of Woods* (1852) p223.
192 Surveyor General to Treasury (Report on the Dean Forest Railways), 15/1/1804, PRO: Crest 8/1.
193 Surveyor General to Treasury, 7/4/1803, PRO: Crest 8/1; and 27/7/1805 (Report on Salaries in the Office of Woods), PRO: Crest 8/2.
194 New Act for the Increase and Preservation of Timber in Dean and New Forests, 48 Geo. III c..72.
195 The Third Report of the Commissioners of Woods. Forests and Land Revenues 1823 p20.

brought under control and virtually eliminated by 1829.[196] Of a total of 2,010.2.6 acres of land which had been enclosed by encroachers up to 1834 only 24 acres had been taken in after 1812.[197] The appointment of permanent Commissioners of Woods, Forests and Land Revenues in 1810 overcame the problem of the Forest's vulnerability to the whims, venality or inattention of particular Surveyors General.[198]

This new administrative energy was not the only influence at work in the Forest. By the time Lord Glenbervie took office, some foreigners had entered the Dean mining industry in partnership with free miners. Although the collapse of the Mine Law Court had produced no short-term consequences of any importance it had deprived the miners of the formal means of disciplining those individuals who were tempted to break the custom. James Teague was thus free to take foreigners into partnership with him in 1796.[199] Since he was a free miner and had properly registered his gale in his own name, there was no question of the decision in the Copper Company's case affecting his works.[200]

Teague built a 'fire engine' at his pit and, more importantly, he laid a small railroad to the River Wye. There is no way of telling precisely what Teague hoped to achieve by doing this but it seems reasonable to speculate that the steam engine would have allowed him to keep water from his mine and, therefore, to work deeper and wider areas of coal. The railroad would have replaced the inefficient method of carrying coal on horses' backs in bags or baskets over roads which were often impassable in winter, reduced the number of men and horses necessary for the work and reduced the cost of the coal at the point of sale on the Wye.

Whatever Teague's ambitions he set a crucial precedent; and one which neither the Forest officers nor the largest part of the free miners liked very much. The officers' vision of the future was clear and it told them that the railroad was a threat and an intrusion. They:

> not only expressed their entire disapprobation of the same, and ordered it to be discontinued, but afterwards, with the

196 Report from the Commissioners of Woods, Forests and Land Revenues to the Lords of the Treasury, recommending measures for ascertaining the Boundaries of the Dean Forest, and for enquiring into the Rights or Claims of Persons calling themselves Free Miners, 25/8/1829. Referred to hereafter as Boundaries Report, 1829.

197 The Second Report of the Dean Forest Commissioners (1834), Appendix No. 3.

198 The functions of the Surveyor General of Land Revenues and of the Surveyor General of Woods and. Forests were vested in the Commissioners by the Act 50 Geo. III, ce.65, in 1810.

199 This account of Teague's railroad is based on the Appendices to *Mining Claims and Disputes*.

200 A gale is a defined area granted for the working of coal or iron ore.

approbation of the Lord Warden, caused the work to be broken up; notwithstanding which, said Teague, assisted by such partners, had thought proper to continue such railroad … if the Crown does not immediately order the same to be thrown up and destroyed the Forest will be laid open to the speculation of every person possessed of money to enter the same without the consent of the Crown or the officers of the Forest, to do what he pleases therein, and terminate in its destruction.[201]

They were aware too that railroads would probably not benefit all miners equally:

Some free miners desired Mr Jones and myself would meet them at the Speech House the 4th of this month to hear their complaints against Mr Teague's partial railroad made against the consent of the officers of the Forest, which was universally condemned, and agreed, if suffered to go on singly would ruin great numbers of families. But several substantial colliers from the Ruardean side, and likewise a few from the Parkend side, thinking a general railroad … would be an advantage to the Forest, and the countries around it, we desired a few colliers to inquire if it could be done without injury to the lower class. They reported that if general railroads were established by an Act of Parliament, in which the rights of the free miners should be confirmed, and that they should have the exclusive right of hauling on the railroads to the Wye and Severn and carrying to the different landing places, as by their laws they have a sole right they thought few carriers would be hurt by it, and the people objecting to it were not many, but since that we have had different lists of free miners, I believe about 150, who have signed against railroads in general, many of whom say it may be a good thing for some of the richer colliers; but as for the poor ones, it will deprive them (they very much fear) of getting the scanty bread they now do…I cannot for one in conscience, join in any Act that is likely to take the bread out of the mouths of the lower class of colliers, who are by much the most numerous. [202]

201 Ibid, Appendix 1, Verderers to Surveyor General, November, 1801.
202 Ibid, Acting Deputy Surveyor to Verderers, 1800.

In this, the question of Teague's railroad has shaded over into that of a general line and there is evidence of a division between the richer and the poorer free miners.

The Forest officers allied themselves for the moment with the poorer miners and appealed to the Treasury Solicitor to prosecute Teague.[203] The Solicitor, however, did nothing. A successful action against Teague might have proceeded on the grounds that the railroad was a nuisance, to be abated, and one which was not sanctioned by customary right.[204] But Teague had argued both that he was entitled to build his line by virtue of the free miners' rights and that the line was not such a nuisance as the road it replaced:

> the miners of the Forest have a right to get coal and ore in the said Forest, time immemorial. They have at the same time enjoyed the privilege of making such roads as the nature and situation of their works required, and this I believe has never in one instance been disputed. Various companies of miners have from time to time made such roads either with earth, wood or stone, as best suited their ability or purpose, without their right to do so being called into question. Indeed the situation of the Forest is such that without this privilege the right of working the mines would be useless, as the low delph seams of coal are situated in such swampy soil that, without the privilege of making roads, almost every pit would be inaccessible in the winter season, whilst the situation of the high delph vein frequently renders necessary to sink shafts or drive levels in the declivity of hills, that without the power to cut roads would be inaccessible either by waggons or beasts of burthen. Upon this ground my Lord, I in the first instance made a road with stone, where my tram road is now made ... but having no hard materials to make it with, it soon became cut to pieces, and persons coming for coal soon began to adopt the general practice of going off the roads upon the swards, till the soil became cut up for one hundred yards wide as a perfect fallow. (The road) became so completely cut up as to be impassable in the winter season and frequently on this account, my coal lay at the pit ... I had no other means than to make my tram road ... You will not be unmindful that whilst envy directs its

203 Ibid, Verderers to Surveyor General, November 1801.
204 Ibid, Appendix No, 2, Attorney General to Surveyor General, November 1803.

shafts against me for making a road that benefits the soil of the Forest, and that in no small degree, all my competitors, and the miners all round the Forest, are still pursuing uninterruptedly the old mode of carriage, and are either making earth, wood or stone roads as best suits them, or else what is far worse, cutting up many acres of land by going on the greens in all directions for want of such roads; and neither the verderers nor keepers think they go in the smallest degree beyond the bounds of their right.[205]

Since "a possible doubt may be raised, especially where the parties may have been at considerable expense, and great mischief may be done by abatement, which upon trial, might turn out not to be justified", [206] the Solicitor procrastinated and allowed Teague's railroad to go uncontested. "Considerable expense", and the property it had created, now counted as an important influence in the decisions which senior servants of the Crown made about Dean Forest.

Teague's adventure encouraged foreigners to attempt a more ambitious scheme. In Hereford, in November 1800 a most impressive gathering of gentlemen, including the Mayor, the Earl of Oxford and the Members of Parliament for the city and country, settled that the most effective way of reducing the price of coal in the city would be to build a railroad "which at the smallest comparative expense would lead to the greatest number of collieries" in the Forest.[207] They commissioned surveys and estimates for the line and began to petition the Parliament and the Treasury for a Railroad Act. Some of the promoters acquired coal holdings along the route of the proposed line and one group of them "formed a connection with Teague etc, and are now preparing to erect a Steam Engine in the Forest, at or near Syrridge, with a view, no doubt, of getting the coal trade and the mines in their own hands".[208]

Once again, the officers predicted the ruin of the Forest and the poorer free miners. The Acting Deputy Surveyor wrote:

the total destruction of the Forest (if considered for a Nursery for Timber) must assuredly follow ... It is intended I understand

205 Ibid, Teague to Treasury Solicitor, 16 October 1803.
206 Ibid, Attorney General to Surveyor General, November 1803.
207 *Gloucester Journal* 17 November 1800.
208 *Mining Claims and Disputes*, Appendix No. I, Acting Deputy Surveyor to Surveyor General 4 April 1802.

to make four principal public roads for the four quarters of the Forest, at the expense of the Company, and collateral railroads to be allowed to be made by individuals into one or other of those principal railroads … Would not the Forest be cut into slips or strips? Take again into consideration the natural inequality of the ground, and as rail or tram roads must be nearly level, you will find deep ditches of long lengths must be cut in some places, and banks raised in others. Must this not be dangerous to travellers who have occasion to pass from one part of the Forest to another? And will it not be an effective barrier to the hauling the Navy Timber from the internal parts of the Forest … yet they will be singularly serviceable to Timber Stealers, who, when the trees are felled and cut into converted lengths for coopers wares, can carry away almost any quantity with the greatest ease and with little fear of detection … as soon as the plan can be settled, powerful steam engines will be erected on those lines; and notwithstanding there is a lure held out to the present miners, that they shall be included in the Act, so as to give them authority to cut collateral rail roads into those principal rail roads, yet as you will know their inability to do so or to cope with monied men, the consequence must be that 1,000 poor honest men (who now but get scarce sufficient to maintain themselves and families) would be ruined, and must throw themselves at the mercy of those foreigners for employ, who when have got all the coal works in the Forest into their own hands will in all probability take care to enrich themselves at the cost of the public.[209]

Glenbervie had this advice before him in 1804 when the Treasury asked him to report on the proposed railroad. He also had memorials in favour of the line from the inhabitants and gentleman of Hereford, from the manufacturers and dyers of woollen cloths in Gloucester and from 52 free miners. A memorial in opposition came from three of the four verderers of the Forest and 406 free miners.[210]

Glenbervie's test of the scheme was its effect on the interests of the Crown as he saw them, but he also gave weight to the possible consequences of the scheme for most of the miners:

209 Ibid, Acting Deputy Surveyor to Verderers, 1800.
210 Ibid, Surveyor General to Treasury, 18 January 1804.

the production and preservation of Navy timber to the extent which has been expected will, I presume, be felt to be of a paramount nature to this declared object of the memorialists, however desirable the attainment of (cheap coal) might be … it will require a period of little less than a century and a permanent, steady and vigorous administration of the Forests during that period … to secure to posterity the most indispensable article for the maintenance of that Navy on which not only the glory and prosperity of the country, but its very safety and existence depend … their project might interfere with the measures which must be adopted in the Forest of Dean with a view to this general plan of prospective improvement … it is most probable that whatever increased emolument may arise from mining in consequence of the present plan, they will chiefly be reaped by strangers, possessed of adequate capitals, colouring the enterprises with the names of privileged persons too poor to avail themselves of their right, and that, as the privilege of each individual miner is claimed to be without stint, a comparatively very small number of them will be sufficient for the purpose of lending their names, while the others, being incapable of entering into competition with the capitalists I have alluded to, will find, their rights no longer of any value.[211]

Accordingly, Glenbervie recommended that the plan not be permitted to proceed. Frustrated in their first attempts to obtain an Act the foreigners adopted another course.[212] They obtained the permission necessary from landowners to build a line from the Severn to the border of the Forest entirely on privately owned land, thus obviating the need for a Railroad Act. This raised the spectre of each mine owner following Teague's example and constructing his own line from the mine to the railhead. The threat this posed to the Forest was incomparably greater than that of an officially sanctioned and regulated general line.

At the same time, the promoters had also altered their plans for a general railway within the Forest so as to remove most of the earlier objections. There would now be two lines, one in the eastern and one in the western valley. They would not be for the restricted use of a few miners but would carry all coal on equal terms. As well provision was to be made for £3,000 of the £35,000 of authorised capital to be reserved

211 Ibid.
212 Surveyor General to Treasury, 15/7/1807, PRO: Crest 8/3; and 5/3/1809, PRO: Crest 8/4.

in £10 non-voting shares for free miners. New surveys had been made of routes which would run over uniformly sloping ground so that cuttings and embankments, or any other destruction of the soil of timber, would be avoided.

More importantly, the lines now came to be seen as a means of implementing the plans to improve the Forest as a nursery and of disciplining the miners who were cast–not as the probable victims of the foreigners–but as the chief threat to the interest of the Crown. If many of the roads in the Forest were closed and a railway built, timber stealing could be limited:

> The lawful occupation of the persons employed will be confined to a narrow compass and that there will be less pretext for their being found with their horses and carts as they now are over the whole tract of forest land.[213]

Inspectors paid for by the railway companies would prevent the use of the line by timber stealers and, a provision in the Railroad Act that no miner who used the line for carriage of coal should be permitted to claim free timber would do away that that abuse. At the same time, the miners' other right, to dig wherever he chose, might also be limited, and regulations framed so as:

> to prevent the opening of new pits at a distance from these railways, in various parts of the Forest where they might interfere with and prevent the enclosures and plantations which may be undertaken under the efficient authority which has now been vested in His Majesty for that purpose.[214]

A clause in the Acts to prevent new lateral lines being opened, or the carriage of coal from any new mine sunk at a distance of more than 100 yards from the main line, without the permission of the Surveyor General, would serve that purpose. Moreover, the railways could pay a substantial licence fee, £400 between them, which would help to finance the enclosures provided for by the Act of 1808. A further provision that the railroads should fence their lines would also fence the enclosures where they marched together.[215]

213 Surveyor General to Treasury, 20/3/07, PRO: Crest 8/3.
214 Surveyor General to Treasury, 5/3/09, PRO: Crest 8/4.
215 Ibid.

On balance, the railroad was now an attractive proposal. It had, by 1808, the support of the Lord Warden and the Forest Officers, and a Bill containing the necessary regulations received Glenbervie's approval in 1809.[216] The orderly development of the Forest as a timber nursery and the protection of the State's interest there demanded an alliance between the State and foreigners. The miners' rights were an anomaly and anachronism, to be curtailed in the interest of efficient administration. In 1807 a group of free miners, presumably those opposed to the railroads and the foreigners, petitioned the Forest Officers for the restoration of the Mine Law Court, but they were ignored.[217]

The Crown and the foreigners did not bear all the responsibility for opening the Forest to capital. James Teague was a free miner and fifty-two other free miners had petitioned in favour of the general railroad. Indeed, all the holdings of foreigners in mines were obtained through the co-operation of free miners. Again, Teague had set the example by taking foreigners into a partnership in a gale registered in his own name. Other free miners did the same. Edward Protheroe, a foreigner and the owner of the single largest group of mines in 1831, described the motives of the free miners and the consequences of their actions in this way:

> As (the) shallow coal was becoming exhausted, the attention of the miners was directed to the deeper coal, which is accessible only by means of the steam-engine, and its expensive pumping and drawing machinery. The free miners took out gales by way of experimental speculation, and in the first instance bargained with strangers possessed of capital for the opening of these works on the terms of holding shares therein themselves; but it was soon found that disagreements and quarrels ensued, and the free miners were obliged to be bought out. It was also found that the expense of opening a deep colliery was so enormous, and the difficulty of establishing a new trade so great, that the first adventurers among foreigners expended their fortunes and received no return to encourage them or others to go on with the system. This was the case with my uncle, who never received back one shilling for his large expenditure. Under these circumstances, he offered his works for sale, and I bought them in conjunction with Mr Waters upon the express condition that he should get conveyed to us all the shares of

216 Ibid.
217 D.F.C., 4, 1835, p.52.

the various free miners who were concerned in the different collieries as partners with him. These shares he purchased for different considerations either in ready money or annuities, some of which I continue to pay to this day ... The free miners then finding that there was no profit to induce strangers to embark their money in the objectionable mode of partnership with them, adopted the system of taking out gales in the most eligible places, and disposing of them to strangers for a small sum of money paid down, and a nominal rent for a long term of years. It is generally acknowledged that these considerations, however small, together with other advantages attending the system, have been much more beneficial to the free miners than their independent speculations. They are mostly working men, and are employed in sinking the pits in managing the machinery, and in working the mines.[218]

The tightening of the Crown's control, the decision to allow railroads, the willingness of some free miners to act as middlemen between the Gaveller and foreigners, and the willingness of foreigners to venture their capital, wrought substantial change in the Forest between 1800 and 1831. The mines passed predominantly into the hands of foreigners who developed them in harness with machines, railroads and, in a few cases, iron furnaces. The total population grew and there was an influx of foreign workmen. At the same time, the uses which its inhabitants could make of the Forest were severely curtailed by the new administrative regime.

The most striking change was in the ownership of the mines. Evidence about this comes from the Award of the Dean Forest Mining Commissioners published in 1841.[219] The Commissioners began to record details of the mines and their ownership in April 1832. Mines were opened between then and 1841, and others changed hands, but these cases have been allowed for in the tables below, which report the state of the industry in April 1832. The Award published the names of the owners of, or shareholders in, each mine, their towns of residence,

218 Ibid, p 24.
219 Award of the Dean Forest Mining Commissioners, 1841, PRO: F17/426. And see: the Commissioners' *Minute Books*, 1838-41, PRO: F20/6; Depositions and other evidences as to rights of mines laid before the Commissioners, 1839-41, PRO: F20/7; and, Claims to Gales and mine workings inquired into by the Commissioners, and evidence heard by them, 1839-41, PRO: F 20/8-10.

Table 8: The number of mines in the Forest of Dean in April 1832 and their relative sizes.

Assessed annual capacity (tons)	Number of mines	Assessed annual capacity (tons)	Number of mines
<250	3	5000–7500	3
250 -500	22	7500–10000	3
500–1000	15	10000–15000	5
1000–2000	17	15000–20000	2
2000–3500	8	20000–25000	4
3500–5000	2	25000–30000	1

Source: Award of the Dean Forest Mining Commissioners, 1841. PRO F 17: 426.

whether they were free miners and, in the case of some foreigners, their occupations. The owners have been put into three groups in the tables: free miners, foreigners and those who lived in the Forest or surrounding parishes but who did not hold as free miners.

The Award also shows the annual tonnage to be taken as the base for calculations of the minimum royalty to be paid to the Crown. This figure represented a fair average assessment of the annual capacity of each mine. Here the figures are not taken to represent absolute production figures but are used as indicators of the relative capacities of each mine and, by grouping, the relative size of holdings of the three groups of owners. The Commissioners heard objections to their awards and classifications before 1841 and these have been allowed for in the tables.

In April 1832 there were 85 mines in Dean whose total assessed capacity was 340,840 tons: 40 of them were assessed at less than 1,000 tons per annum, and the balance at between 1,000 and 30,000 tons. (See Table 8)

The free miners were no longer the exclusive or even the principal owners of the mines. Acting alone, or in partnership with other free miners, they held only twenty mines or 34.10 % of the total. Foreigners now held thirty-one mines and other foresters seven: 36.47 % and 8.24 % of the total respectively. Mixed ownership, by miners and foreigners together, by foreigners and other foresters and by miners and other foresters, accounted for the balance of 21.18 %. (See Table 9) When allowance is made for the relative capacities of the mines, the foreigners

Table 9: Ownership of the forest of Dean Mines in April 1832.

Owner	Number of mines	% of total mines	Assessed capacity	% of total capacity
Free Miners	29	34.1	66,520	19.51
Foreigners	31	36.47	176,320	51.73
Other Forest	7	8.24	16,240	4.77
Free Miners and Foreigners	7	8.24	65,240	19.14
Foreigners and Other Forest	4	4.70	4,160	1.22
Free Miners and Other Forest	7	8.24	12,360	3.63
Totals	**85**	**100**	**340,840**	**100.00**

Source: Award of the Dean Forest Mining Commissioners, 1841. PRO F 17: 426.

are seen to have had a much more dominant position. (See Table 10) Though the free miners controlled, completely, 34.10 % of the mines, they had only 19.51 % of total capacity: foreigners, without partners, controlled 51.73 %. After distributing the portions of the mixed partnership mines, the proportion of capacity held by free miners increases to 27.57 %. But the dominance of the foreigners is even more apparent. They controlled 66.43 % of capacity. Other foresters held 6 %.

As well as this inequality between the different groups, there were inequalities within them. (See Table 10) All told, 132 men had shares in the Forest mines in 1832: 56 were free miners, 43 were foreigners and 33 were other foresters. Of the 132, 98 or 74.25 % each had shareholdings which were of no more than 1,000 tons capacity. Those shares were worth only 8.93 % of the total Forest capacity. About one-quarter of the shareholders had total holdings of more than 1,000 tons each. They accounted for 92.07 % of total capacity. The same pattern was apparent within each group. Among the miners, 23.22 % had 88.54 % of the capacity held by miners. For foreigners, the figures are 32.56 % and 95.13 % and, for other foresters, 21.21 % and 74.34 % respectively.

Inequalities had developed in other ways as well. The foreigners, as might be expected, had more machinery at work for them than the free miners. Of the seventeen pumping and winding engines for which the

Table 10: Forest of Dean miners 1832: The number of shareholders and the size of total shareholders within each ownership group.

Free miners				
Size of total shareholding (tons)*	Number of shareholders	% of shareholders	Total capacity (tons)**	% of total capacity
< 250	27	48.21	2,895	3.08
250–500	11	19.64	3,839	4.09
500–1000	5	8.93	4,038	4.29
> 1000	13	23.22	83,202	88.54
Totals	56	100	93,974	100

% of total capacity   **27.57 %**

Foreigners				
Size of total shareholding (tons)*	Number of shareholders	% of shareholders	Total capacity (tons)	% of total capacity
< 250	15	34.88	2,417	1.07
250–500	6	13.95	1,870	0.82
500–1000	8	18.61	6,750	2.98
> 1000	14	32.56	215,387	95.13
Totals	43	100	226,424	

% of total capacity   **66.43 %**

Other forest				
Size of total shareholding (tons)*	Number of shareholders	% of shareholders	Total capacity (tons)	% of total capacity
< 250	18	54.55	2,502	12.24
250–500	7	21.21	2,143	10.48
500–1000	1	3.03	600	2.95
> 1000	7	21.21	15,197	74.34
Totals	33	100	20,442	100

% of total Capacity   **6%**

Totals				
Size of total shareholding (tons)*	Number of shareholders	% of shareholders	Total capacity (tons)	% of total capacity
< 250	60	45.36	7,814	2.29
250–500	24	18.18	7,852	2.30
500–1000	14	10.61	11,388	3.34
> 1000	34	25.75	313,786	92.07
Totals	132	100	340,840	100

% of total capacity   **100%**

* In tons of assessed capacity.
** Total capacity held by the shareholders in each size category.
Source: Award of the Dean Forest Mining Commissioners, 1841. PRO F 17: 426.

Crown had granted licences before 1831, fifteen belonged to foreigners.[220] Eleven of the machines belonged to the one man, Edward Protheroe. By 1832 he had twelve. They allowed him to push his mines from the outcrop into the deep coal:

> The depth of my principal pits at Park End and Bilson varies from about 150 to 200 yards. That of my new gales, for which I have engine licences, is estimated at from 250 to 300 yards. I have 12 steam engines varying from 12 to 140 horse power, nine or ten of which are at work, the whole amounting to 500 horsepower.[221]

It is probable, however, that the engines were of value to men other than their owners, because they drained off much larger areas of coal than those belonging to the mines in which they were installed. Free miners, as well as foreigners, pleaded in evidence before the Dean Forest Commissioners in 1832 that if the foreigners stopped the engines no one else would be able to work since the field would be drowned.[222] The machines probably made possible substantial increases in output. According to an estimate made by the Deputy Surveyor in 1818, the output had averaged about 70,000 tons a year from 1800 to 1806, about

220 Award of the Mining Commissioners, Third Schedule.
221 D.T.C., 4, p.25.
222 Ibid, p.15.

100,000 tons a year from 1807 to 1816 and was in 1817, 130,000 tons. The field's production had thus almost doubled between 1800 and 1817 and probably doubled again by 1831.[223]

Foreigners dominated the railroads as well as the mines. The lines sanctioned by Glenbervie's decision in 1809, the Severn and Wye and the Bullo Pill, opened in 1810.[224] A third line running from Lydbrook to Monmouth opened in 1812.[225] Once again Protheroe was the leading man. He had about half the shares in the Severn and Wye Company and acted as its chairman in most of the years before 1831.[226] When the Bullo Pill line collapsed financially in 1826 Protheroe bought out the whole of their interests. He kept for himself the Great Bilson colliery which the company had opened to provide traffic and sold the line to the Forest of Dean Railway Company which he formed for the purpose and of which he became chairman.[227] Protheroe thus came to control the carriage of coal to the eastern side of the Forest. This was the source of later complaints about a railroad 'monopoly'. [228]

The Monmouth line was entirely in the hands of foreigners and was the only one to serve the western side of the Forest. Some of its shareholders were foreigners who owned coal mines in Dean but most were inhabitants of Monmouth.[229] The free miners' lack of control of the railroads might not have been a great problem if the lines had been operated as a subordinate service for the mines. But, Protheroe wrote, "the truth is that the only persons who have ever ventured to open deep coal works have done it to serve their interests as railroad proprietors". [230] Protheroe might have been able to strike a balance between the wish to derive profit from the railroads and the wish to derive profit from the mines. For those who depended principally on the mines, a price for the carriage of coal which would provide the railway companies with a good return could only be a source of grievance.

Some of the mines were linked with iron furnaces as well as with railroads. In 1831 the Cinderford Iron Company had two blast furnaces, the Forest of Dean Iron Company had two at its Park End works and

223 Return respecting the Mines in Dean Forest, *Parliamentary Papers*, 1818, Vol. XV.
224 *Gloucester Journal* 21 May 1810, 4 June 1810 and 11 June 1810.
225 *Gloucester Journal* 24 August 1812.
226 D.F.C., 4, p.22.
227 Ibid, p.23; and, H W Paar, *The Great Western Railway in Dean,* 2nd edition (Newton Abbot, David and Charles, 1971) Ch.2.
228 See below Chapter 5.
229 Paar, *The Great Western Railway in Dean,* Chapter 8.
230 D.F.C., 4, p.24.

Table 11: Coal holdings of the owners and lessees of Forest of Dean furnaces in april 1832.

Name	Furnace	Mines	Assessed capacity (tons)
Edward Protheroe	Parkend	6 groups of mines and 1/4 share in another	98,387
David Mushet	Dark Hill	3 mines and 1/4 share in another	3,840
John James	Parkend	I mine	1,480
Moses Teague	Parkend and Cinderford	3 mines	19,600
Moses Teague and William Montague	Parkend and Cinderford	I mine: Teague (1/3) and Montague (2/3)	24,000
Moses Teague and William Crawshay		1 mine	24,000
Cinderford Iron Co.		1 mine	1,800
Total			**173,107**

Source: Award of the Dean Forest Mining Commissioners, 1841. PRO F 17: 426.

David Mushet had another at Dark Hill. [231] Mushet owned as well an iron ore mine at Oakwood. The members of the Cinderford Company were Moses Teague, a free miner, William Montague, the owner of an iron foundry in Gloucester, and two other foreigners. Montague and John James of Lydney leased the Park End furnace from Edward Protheroe in 1825 and employed Moses Teague as their manager from 1827.

William Crawshay, the Welsh ironmaster, had no furnace in Dean but shared ownership of a mine with Moses Teague. Crawshay acquired control of the Cinderford works by 1841. This small group of men who had an interest in iron furnaces together owned about half the Forest's coal capacity and dominated the railroads. (See table 11). Edward Protheroe, of the Severn and Wye and Forest of Dean railroads, had mine holdings amounting to 98,387 tons or 28.87 % of total Forest capacity, owned the Park End furnace and premises, and supplied coal from his mines to both iron companies. Mushet owned three coal mines as well as his furnace

231 Hart, *The Industrial History of the Dean*, Chapter 3 and Nicholls, *Iron Making*, 224-229.

and iron mine. He was chairman of the Severn and Wye in 1823 and had shares in the Monmouth mine. Teague, Crawshay, Montague, James and the Cinderford Iron Company had another seven mines and a share in one more. Together with Protheroe and Mushet they owned all the six mines with a capacity of more than 20,000 tons and, in total, 173,107 tons or 50.79 % of the Forest's capacity. (See Table 11).

So far as Forest industry had diversified, and integrated holdings in the railroads, the mines and the iron furnaces had begun to emerge, foreigners and most especially Edward Protheroe, were in a position of control. Taken all in all, as the Dean Forest Commissioners concluded it was clear that "the monopoly and the customary workings, are practically at an end". [232]

Inevitably the growth and concentration of the mining industry created a large class of wage labourers:

> By the greater outlay of capital, which has taken place under this new system, the custom of working by partners and apprentices has been nearly abolished, and has been succeeded by the practice of working the mines by hired labourers.[233]

There is no way of telling precisely how many men were employed in the Forest, but some rough indicators are available. In their fourth report, the Dean Forest Commissioners listed the names of 947 men who claimed to be free miners.[234] Of these 56 were proprietors in a greater or lesser degree. Allowing for them, there were about 891 free miners in the Forest in 1835. This, the Commissioners reported, was an underestimate since some men had not registered.[235] There were as well the foreign workmen. Again, there is no way of telling how many of them there were, but, in 1831, of the 1530 families in the Forest, about one fifth had settlements in parishes beyond the Hundred of St. Briavels, that is they were foreigners.[236] Adding one quarter to the Commissioner's list gives a total of 1,114 employed men. There were as well 143 quarrymen, which brings the total to 1,257. This is still an underestimate of employees since it does not allow for inhabitants of the Forest who were not free miners, foreigners or quarrymen or who worked on the railroads or in

232 D.F.C., 4, p.10.
233 Ibid, p 8.
234 Ibid, Appendix No. 2.
235 Ibid, p 8.
236 D.F.C., 3, p.5

Table 12: Population of the Forest of Dean and the hundred of st briavels 1801-1831.

	Census Year				Percentage increase 1801–1831
	1801	1811	1821	1831	
Forest of Dean	3,325	4,073	5,535	7,014	110.97
Parishes	12,272	14,637	17,084	20,064	63.49
Total for the Hundred of St Briavels	**15,597**	**18,710**	**22,619**	**27,078**	**73.61**

Source: Population Abstracts, 1801–1831

Table 13:

Parish	No. of Families	Percentage
Hundred of St Briavels	1,193	77.97
Foreigners	325	21.24
No Settlement	12	0.79
Total No. of Families	**1,530**	**100**

Source: The Third Report of the Dean Forest Commissioners, June 13, 1835, p 5.

the ironworks. All told there were probably between 1,000 and 2,000 employed men in the Forest around 1831, of whom between 400 and 500 worked for Edward Protheroe.

With the growth of industry and the workforce, there went an increase in population. The census of 1801 recorded 3,325 people in Dean. That of 1831 recorded 7,014 people: an increase of 110.97 %. (See Table 12). Apart from natural increase, population growth followed from the continued movement of people into the Forest from the surrounding parishes. There had been as well the influx of foreigners noted above. Of the 1,530 families living in Dean in 1831, 1,193 had settlements in parishes within the Hundred of St Briavels. The balance of 325, or 21.24 %, had come from remote parishes, beyond the border of the Hundred. (See Table 13). The absence of references to foreign workmen in the eighteenth century and the complaints of miners around 1831 about the importation of foreign workmen by coal owners suggest that the foreigners in the population were relative newcomers.[237]

237 See below Ch. V.

Table 14: Encroachments in the Forest of Dean, 1787 and 1834.

	1787	1834
Number of Patches	899	1,592
Land Encroached (acres. rods. perches)	1,385.3.21	2,010.2.6
Average Area per Patch (acres. rods. perches)	1.2.07	1.1.2
Number of Cottages	593	1,380
Average Area Per Cottage (acres. rods. perches)	2.1.14	1.1.33

The Second Report of the Dean Forest Commissioners, 1 May 1834, Appendix 3.
William and Abraham Driver, *Particulars of a Survey of the Forest of Dean in the County of Gloucester*, PRO, F16, 31.

The uses which this expanded population could make of the Forest had been strictly curtailed by 1831. The new efficiency of Forest management imposed a number of restrictions on the inhabitants. With the enclosures provided for by the Act of 1808 properly maintained and policed by officers who had no perquisites or fines to encourage them to ignore their duty, the foresters were not able to pasture animals in the woods all year round. In winter they could maintain only the pigs and sheep their small patches of ground would support. Timber stealing probably disappeared as an organised, open activity as a result of the closure of roads, the inspection of the railroads and the close supervision of the Forest by the first Deputy Surveyor of the new regime, Edward Machen.[238]

The foresters were still able to benefit from the timber and wood in a number of ways: Timothy Mountjoy's account of fern burning and bark stripping in the early years of Machen's term of office referred to above in Chapter 2, indicated clearly that there was still an opportunity for women and young children to contribute to family incomes. Significantly, though, Mountjoy referred to their "making wages". These activities were probably carried out now by people in Machen's employment rather than by the foresters on their own account.

As might be expected the increase in population together with the restriction of encroachments resulted in a shift in the pattern of use

238 Boundaries Report, 1829, p.2.

Table 15: Encroachments and cottages in the Forest of Dean in 1834.

Number of cottages held by each encroacher	Area of land held by each encroacher in acres						
	0–0.5	0.5–1	1–5	5–10	10–15	Totals	%
0	246	101	114	13	6	480	30.16
1	371	203	320	30	1	925	58.10
2	26	31	66	9	4	136	8.54
3	6	4	20	1	1	32	2.01
4	-	-	10	-	1	11	0.69
5	-	-	4	1	1	6	0.38
6	-	-	-	-	1	1	0.06
7	-	-	1	-	-	1	0.06
Totals	649	339	535	54	15	1592	
%	40.77	21.30	33.60	3.30	0.94		100

The Second Report of the Dean Forest Commissioners, 1 May 1834, Appendix 3.
William and Abraham Driver, *Particulars of a Survey of the Forest of Dean in the County of Gloucester*, PRO, F16, 31.

of the enclosed land from gardening and grazing to housing. In 1834 there were 1,592 patches of land with 1,380 cottages: an average of 1.1.2 (acres. rods. perches) per encroachment, (Table 14) a quarter of an acre less than the equivalent average for 1787 of 1.2.07 acres. More striking was the decrease of almost an acre in the average encroached area per cottage: from 2.1.14 acres in 1787 to 1.1.33 in 1834. There were again in 1834 people who held land but no cottage and others who had more than one cottage. (Table 15). As well, individual holdings ranged in size up to fifteen acres. Most, however, in 1834 as in 1787, had less than five acres and one cottage or none.

Over the forty-six years, the proportion of encroachers holding between ten and fifteen acres of land had increased 114.29 %, from seven to fifteen people. (See Table 16). This represented only a small increase in the proportion holding that many acres: from 0.77 to 0.94 % of the total number of encroachers. However, the proportion holding less than one acre increased from 53.17 % to 62.07 %. That holding between one and ten acres fell from 46.06 % to 36.99 %. This, together with the decline

Table 16: Encroached land and cottages in the Forest of Dean, 1787 and 1834.

Encroached land				
Area held by each encroacher in acres	Encroachers 1787		Encroachers 1834		% increase in each category 1787–1834
	Number	%	Number	%	
0–0.5	305	33.93	649	40.77	112.79
0.5–1	173	19.24	339	21.30	95.95
1–5	377	41.94	535	33.60	41.90
5–10	37	4.12	54	3.39	45.95
10–15	7	0.77	15	0.94	114.29
Totals	899	100	1,592	100	77.07

Cottages				
Number of cottages held by each encroacher	Cottages 1787		1834		% increase in each category 1787 -1834
	Number	%	Number	%	
0	405	45.05	480	30.16	18.52
1	421	46.83	925	58.10	119.71
2	51	5.67	136	8.54	166.66
3	21	2.34	32	2.01	52.33
4	1	0.11	11	0.69	-
5	-	-	6	0.38	-
6	-	-	1	0.06	-
7	-	-	1	0.06	-
Totals	899	100	1,592	100	

The Second Report of the Dean Forest Commissioners, 1 May 1834, Appendix 3.
William and Abraham Driver, *Particulars of a Survey of the Forest of Dean in the County of Gloucester*, PRO, F16, 31.

in the acreage per cottage, suggests that there was a more intensive use of the available land for housing and a shift towards smaller holdings of land.

The change in the amount of land held in the names of those who were not cottage holders points to the same conclusion. These were most probably people who lived as tenants or as members of a family in a cottage owned by someone else. In 1834, 480 holdings were of that sort: an increase of 18.53 % over the 405 of 1788. But the proportion of encroachments in this category fell from 45.0 % to 30.16 %. In other words, the average amount of land comprised in family holdings or held by tenants was decreasing. The alternative explanation, that the number of tenants was decreasing cannot be supported.

In 1787, 96 cottages out of 593 or 16.21 %, were held as second, third or fourth cottages. By 1831 there were 268. A further 82 cottages belonging to churches, to gentlemen who lived beyond the Forest's borders and to the coal and iron companies: a total of 350 out of 1,462, or 23.93 % of all cottages.[239]

In the space of forty years then, within the lifetimes of some of those who were miners in 1788, and of the boys who were working their freedom, the old system in the Forest had disappeared. The mining industry had passed in the main from the hands of a relatively large group of working proprietors of small-scale co-operative pits into those of a small group of men, mostly foreigners, who brought with them the steam engine, deep mining, railroads and iron furnaces. Most of the inhabitants of the Forest were now wage earners. The population had grown and there had been an influx of foreign workmen. Administrative changes had curtailed the inhabitants' opportunity to use the Forest for timber stealing, pasture and cottages. The increase in population and the restriction of encroachments resulted in a more intensive use of land for houses rather than for gardens or orchards and had increased the proportion of tenants rather than owners of cottages.

None of these tendencies, of course, had entirely done away with the old practices. Fifty-six free miners still had shares in mines and most of the inhabitants had small patches of land. But the horizon of economic opportunity had contracted sharply. A man might still register a gale but had to contemplate the possibility of competition with Edward Protheroe and the others who had the advantages of capital and machines. He might still steal timber, and probably did on a small scale,

239 D.F.C., Appendix 3.

but the open exploitation of the Forest permitted under the old system was no longer possible as half of it indeed was fenced off from him. In the processes which brought about these changes three factors had been of critical importance: the determination of the State to reassert its control; the expediency for the State of an alliance with the foreigners; and the willingness of some free miners to act as middlemen between the foreigners and the Gaveller or to take foreigners as partners.

Chapter Five

The Miners' Rights

Having discussed the long-term influences which had been at work in the society and economy of the Forest, we may now examine the more immediate background to the miners' riot. In 1828, the Commissioners of Woods took the first steps towards a further limitation of the free miners' rights, by legislation, in a manner which would favour the foreigners.

This provoked a campaign by the miners for the revival of the old Mine Law Court and the restoration of the miners' exclusive privileges. The riot in 1831, this chapter will argue, developed from that campaign. That being so the riot should not be interpreted as a limited anti-enclosure movement but seen in the broader context of conflict between the native miners and cottagers, on the one hand, and the State and the foreign capitalists on the other.

At the end of the 1820's, the Crown had taken yet further steps to rationalise its administration of the Forest by initiating a Bill to define and limit the miners' privileges. The restrictive provisions of the various Railroad Acts had satisfactorily curbed the miners' right to take timber at will but there remained their right to dig for coal wherever they wished. The officers in the Forest, and by implication the Crown, had long recognised that right in practice. The Commissioners of 1788 had concluded, however, that, despite the Copper Company case, the miners could probably not legally sustain their claim to special privileges against the Crown.[240] The absence of the records of the old Mine Law Court was crucial because without the documents the miners could base their case only on what was remembered by individuals and over time this had become confused and contradictory. The Book of Dennis contained a basic outline of the rights but said nothing about the regulations made by the Mine Court. To those concerned with the administration of the Forest as a nursery, the miners' rights were obscure, ill-defined, probably illegal, certainly unproductive of revenue and potentially destructive of the Forest.

As early as 1807 the Surveyor General had insisted to the Treasury that there should be some examination of the rights:

240 See L.R.C., 1788, pp.1-34.

It must be highly necessary to institute some vigorous enquiry into the claims of the persons calling themselves free miners, both with respect to the right of mining, and the use of timber for their works, as there can be no doubt but more mines will be sunk, and more produce drawn from the Forest after the establishment of the proposed railways and if they shall continue to be supplied with timber ... the whole of the Beech in the Forest must be exhausted. It would certainly be very difficult, and perhaps impracticable to obtain complete possession of the mines, from the lawless description of the persons by whom they are now worked.[241]

This plan emerged again in 1828 and in December of that year, the Treasury ordered the Commissioners of Woods to begin an inquiry into the "nature and extent of the customary rights exercised by the free miners in the Forest of Dean and to as what evidence can be adduced in support of those rights".[242] The consequent report, which the Commissioners sent to the Treasury in 1829, set out the rights and privileges in a fairly complete form, but it adopted a hostile tone. "There has long been occasion to observe", they wrote, "the great injury that has arisen to the interests of His Majesty, and daily continues to arise, as well as the loss and inconvenience to individuals having invested their property in mining speculations in the Forest, from the undefined and conflicting claims of the persons calling themselves free miners". The opinions of the best law authorities "who have been consulted on the subject are, that the exercise of such claims, in the manner and to the unlimited extent urged, cannot now be legally maintained".[243] Having stated the probable answer to the question about the legality of the miners' rights the report urged that:

competent professional persons be appointed under the authority of an Act of Parliament, with all the power given in such cases, to proceed both by the examination of intelligent witnesses, on the spot, and upon oath, and by the inspection of any deeds, writings or other legal testimony which they may be able to obtain; and thereupon to report what rights the miners shall have appeared to have acquired either by grant,

241 Surveyor General to Treasury, 15/7/1807, PRO: Crest 8/3.
242 Treasury to Commissioners of Woods, 15/12/1828, PRO: Crest 8 16.
243 Boundaries Report, 1829, p.3.

prescription or otherwise; and if it shall be found that their claims cannot be maintained to the extent now sought for, then in what manner it may be expedient that they should be limited and defined by legislative enactment.[244]

Earlier, in 1818, the Commissioners had declared that "we are not in Possession of any Charters, Grants or Documents (concerning the free miners' rights) nor have we been able to ascertain that any such documents exist".[245] The records of the Mine Law Court, of course, did not come to light until 1832. That being so, all that remained of substance in the Commissioners recommendations was to discover an expedient manner of defining and limiting the rights by legislation.

Despite the foreigners' dominance of the coal industry in Dean, the free miners' rights were not entirely valueless. Some of the miners, an unknown number, had turned the new order of things to their own account. By acting as middlemen between the Gaveller and the foreigners some miners had secured an annual royalty.[246] If the foreigners wished to extend their holdings, as things stood they had to employ a free miner. But if the title in the mineral rights was no longer restricted to free miners then the advantage some had as middlemen, or would have in the future, would be lost. There remained as well the fact that some free miners did have small mines of their own. They stood as a model of opportunity for those who did not. Most of the miners were wage labourers but, so long as the restrictive customs applied, there was the possibility that they might become proprietors. After 1826 some might have imagined that this was a real possibility.

About that time the Purton Pill railroad scheme took shape. This line was designed to run from Purton Pill on the Severn up to roughly the centre of the Forest at Foxes Bridge. It was to run about midway between the existing Severn and Wye and Bullo Pill lines, across an area of coal which was largely undeveloped.[247] The scheme thus offered new opportunity for free miners to acquire gales, along a railroad that would make the gales worth having. Little is known about this scheme except that it was promoted by Moses Teague, a free miner.[248]

Teague was one of the few free miners who had prospered in partnership with the foreigners. The son of that James Teague who had

244 Ibid.
245 Return respecting the Miners in Dean Forest, Parliamentary Papers, 1818, volume XV, p.99.
246 D.F.C., 4, p.24.
247 See Paar, The Great Western Railway, Chapter 10 and G.H.O. O/rum: 124-125.
248 Ibid.

caused so much difficulty with his small railroad in 1796. Moses Teague described himself, in 1832 as a "Coal Surveyor and Engineer". [249] As we noticed in Chapter Four, he was a proprietor of one iron company and the manager of another. He owned three coal mines, including the Foxes Bridge mine.[250] The railroad was probably yet a further stage in Teague's entrepreneurial career.

For Teague, and other free miners, the miners' rights were probably of considerable value given the possibility that the railroad scheme might succeed. They would give the free miners the first option on the newly opened coal area. That would be of value even if a miner's purpose in registering a gale were only later to sell it or lease it to someone else. If the free miners' rights were abolished, of course, foreigners would have as much opportunity as miners to acquire title to the coal.

The Bill which was prepared as a result of the Commissioners' report and presented to the House of Commons in October 1829 was not solely concerned with the miners' right to dig coal. It contained as well an instruction to the Commissioners to be appointed under it to:

> report the dates, value and other particulars of all other purprestures, encroachments and trespasses in and upon the soil of His Majesty within the said Forest, in all cases in which it shall not clearly appear to the said Commissions that a good title can be established against the Crown.[251]

The anxiety which this provision provoked found expression in an article in the *Monmouthshire Merlin:*

> That laws framed under circumstances which no longer exist cannot be rightly available under the influence and power that all laws should possess; must be self-evident; and therefore we approve of so much of this Bill as tends to define the rights of the foresters amongst themselves, because we think it at once conducive to their separate interests and their unanimity and prosperity as a body. Men and their political interests are necessarily open to those alterations which time and circumstances require, and thus it can be readily imagined that

249 D.F.C., p.28.
250 Award of the Dean Forest Mining Commissioners, 1841.
251 A Bill for Ascertaining the Boundaries of the Forest of Dean, and for inquiring into the Rights and Privileges claimed by the Free Miners of the Hundred of St Briavels, and for other purposes, *Parliamentary Papers*, Vol. 2, 1830.

the same Forest laws which were framed, and fairly applied perhaps a century ago, when coal was procured at little or no expense, now require both revision and correction under the expenditure of immense sums to realise the same results. But from the enactments of this Bill, much fear is entertained that an attempt will be made to oust the occupiers of small pieces of ground, tenements, etc, who, if not retaining their possession by any positive law, have nevertheless done so under the manifest conviction of those who might have interfered; that if any counteracting law did exist, there was much more honour, and policy too, perhaps, in submitting to its breach than enforcing its rigid observance.[252]

The Bill thus potentially threatened cottagers in general as well as the free miners in particular. The Commissioners probably did not intend this inquiry to be directed against foreigners. There had after all been considerable co-operation between the Crown and the capitalists. So much so that Protheroe was able to argue that the Crown had in practice established the foreigners' title to their coal:

In what way has the sanction of the Crown officers been given?

In the first place by their making the Crown a party to the different Acts of Parliament for forming railways in the Forest at the expense of the foreigners (as they are called), who held coal and iron mines, with whom they concerted all these clauses in the said Acts designed to give security to the Royal timber and which have produced incalculable benefit to the Crown property, this security being only attainable through our intervention.

Secondly, by their entering the various conveyances and leases of gales from free miners to or for foreigners, in the Crown books, and receiving the rents and dues from the foreigners.

Thirdly, by their granting after such transfers, licences for engines and railroads, etc., directly to such foreigners describing the mines or works as the property of the said foreigners.

252 *Monmouthshire Merlin* 5 June 1830.

Fourthly, by their lending to the foreigners so possessed of works in the Forest the protection and direct interference of the power of the Crown in suits against free miners illegally interrupting the proceedings, or injuring the property of the foreigners, as occurred in my own case in the year 1824, when the Attorney General filed a Bill in the Exchequer for my protection against the Churchway Company of free miners and obtained an injunction on the proceedings, which was acquiesced in and obeyed.

Fifthly, by the written explanation and declaration from Lord Lowther, when Chief Commissioner, to myself in a letter dated 8th June 1830, written in answer to a formal inquiry on my part. His Lordship's words are, "With respect to works carried on under licence from the Crown, we can have no intention of disputing a right exercised under such a licence, as that would be to quarrel with the title which we ourselves confer".[253]

Protheroe's letter to Lowther, and the reply to it, indicate that they had discussed the problem of his title to the mines he worked. Discussions between them had probably gone on well before that. A letter from the Commissioners of Woods to the Treasury in 1828 approving engine licences for Protheroe, states that he had agreed to a limited form of licence because of the necessity at some time "soon, to investigate fully the respective rights and interests of the Crown, and of the Coal and other mining works".[254] Moreover, the Commissioners' report in 1829 had, referred sympathetically to "the loss and inconvenience to individuals having invested their property in mining speculations in the Forest, that is "individuals" as distinct from free miners.[255]

Protheroe and other foreigners might indeed have hoped to benefit from legislation limiting the miners' rights. There is a clue to this in the correspondence between Protheroe and the Commissioners concerning the drafting of the Dean Forest (Mines) Act of 1838.[256] This Act was the direct consequence of the inquiries of the Dean Forest Commissioners who were appointed as a result of the 1829 report and the Bill which followed it. One point stands out in Protheroe's comments that is whatever

253 D.F.C., 4, p.23.
254 Commissioners of Woods to Treasury, 11/8/1828, PRO: Crest 8/16.
255 Boundaries Report, 1829, p.1.
256 Preparation of the Dean Forest (Mines) Act, 1838, PRO: F3/837 and see below pp.73 -75.

other advantages might arise from the closer regulation of the free miners, property in the mineral rights had to be made real and not personal. That is to say, mineral rights had to be held on the same legal basis as any other property and be transferable through sale or lease and, therefore, be capable of use as mortgage security. Mineral rights held by the free miners were personal in that they accrued to individuals and were contingent upon birth and having worked in the mines. Though miners' rights had in fact been leased, sold and mortgaged, the property was not secure:

> However good our titles may be for possession, we know that they are not legally marketable, unless in our own district where the whole system is known and understood. A variety of causes may render sales of importance to us, and for one, I should be quite content to make some sacrifice of profit, by a small addition to the Crown rent in return for a clear title to a definite extent of local property.[257]

A new Act, in order to confer clear title, would have to remove the need to use miners as middlemen and to declare the legality of the foreigners' holdings. That would require the elimination of the free miners' exclusive right to the coal. The interests of the Crown and the foreigners were thus compatible. It is unlikely that Protheroe and Lowther had not discovered this before 1830.

Opposition from some of the miners had begun while the Commissioners were still preparing their report. The miners did:

> by memorial addressed to the Duke of Beaufort, the present Constable of St Briavels, and to our Board, petition to have the Mine Law Court revived; and on this subject, we are at present in communication with the Law Officers of the Crown.[258]

> On 11 June, the day before the Bill, copies of which had circulated in the Forest, was due to be considered in Committee, the House of Commons received a petition from Warren James: a native and free miner of the Hundred of St Briavels ... taking notice of the Bill ... and praying to be heard by his Counsel against the same.[259]

257 D.F.C., 4, p.26.
258 Boundaries Report, 1829, p.2.
259 *House of Commons Journal*, Vol.85 (Session 1830), 11/6/1830.

This is the first appearance in the evidence of the 'Captain' of the riot. Clearly, his part in the affair was more than the temporary leadership of a mob of rioters. James, a free miner and the working proprietor of a small mine, had watched the development of the Bill, had consulted a solicitor and had gone so far as to petition to be heard before Parliament. *The Gloucester Journal* later reported that the miners had "levied large sums among themselves to support James".[260] At about this time too, another edition of the Book of Dennis appeared in the Forest. All this suggests strongly that some of the miners at least were conducting a definite and deliberate campaign to restore their old privileges in response to an apparent campaign by the State to remove them altogether. There is no evidence, however, that James' petition was allowed or that it in any way altered the progress of the Bill. The other petitions, for the restoration of the Court, had similarly little impact. The Commissioners concluded that "it would be very inexpedient to establish such a jurisdiction at the present day".[261]

It is appropriate at this point to turn again to the riot, which we may now see, despite the paucity of the evidence, as something more complex than a 'local anti-enclosure movement'. The Commissioners' Bill was due to be read again on 23 June 1831, a fortnight after the riot began.[262] The riot we have already noted did not break out spontaneously but was the result of forethought and planning by James, the man who had petitioned to be heard against the Bill. James had composed a notice, submitted it to the printer at Coleford and then distributed it in advance of a stipulated meeting date. It seems reasonable to infer that James provoked the disturbance in an attempt to influence Parliament's reception of the Bill and to bring the miners' demands forcibly before it. This interpretation is consistent with some other fragments of evidence which we have about the riot. What the miners wanted, *The Gloucester Journal* reported, was "the restitution of the Forest and Mine Courts".[263] And again, among "the numerous ills the free miners have been made to suffer prior to the 8th day of June" listed in an anonymous 'explanation' of the riot, which *The Forester* published, was a complaint that:

> His Grace the Duke of Beaufort, as Constable of the Castle at
> St Briavels and Lord Chief Ranger of the Forest, has been for

260 *The Gloucester Journal* 25 June 1831.
261 Boundaries Report, 1829, p.2.
262 *House of Commons Journal*, Vol.1 (Session 1831), 25/6/1831.
263 *The Gloucester Journal* 25 June 1831.

nearly three years past trifling with the patience and miseries of the free miners by denying their just demands of opening their free miners' Courts according to their ancient rights and privileges, and which they usually enjoyed from time immemorial, the grants made to them by Edward the 3rd.[264]

This suggests in other words, that just as the second reading of the Bill was a stage in the Commissioner's campaign to limit the miners' rights, so the riot was a stage in the miners' counter-campaign to revive the rights and the old Court. Opposition to the Bill offers a reason for the presence at the enclosures of John Harris, a self-described 'yeoman' or cottager, along with James, the small proprietor, and others who were workmen in the mines.[265]

The Bill offers a reason too for the encouragement which, Beaufort reported to the Home Office, some of the "free miners of property" gave to the rioters.[266] Could those free miners have been the promoters of the Purton railroad? Only one scrap of evidence survives to suggest that this may have been so. A report of the riot in *The Times* read in part:

Whether these disturbances are to end here, time only will develop: some of the more violent are for proceeding to other acts of violence; the railways which intersect the Forest in every direction, and the turnpike gates, are rumoured to be the next objects of attack, but the leaders appear to consider that the work for which they assembled was finished last night.[267]

This suggests a difference of opinion between the leaders and the led about the railroads. As we shall see below, some of the rioters identified the foreigners and their railroads as the source of unemployment and distress in the Forest. Why should the leaders have been unwilling to go on to tear up the railroads? That would make sense if the leaders had some connection with the Purton Pill promoters and had an interest in not tearing up railroads indiscriminately. The Purton Pill scheme offers an explanation, too, of the rumours of plot and conspiracy which appeared in the newspapers. Perhaps the malign being in London was

264 *The Forester* 4 August 1831.
265 *The Gloucester Journal* 11 June 1831 and 25 June 1831 and *Monmouthshire Merlin* 11 June 1831.
266 Beaufort to Home Office, 15 June 1831, PRO: H.O. 52/12.
267 *The Times* 14 June 1831.

James' solicitor. His friends were the railroad promoters and the ancient source of royal authority was the Book of Dennis. None of this is based on substantial, satisfactory evidence. But it at least imposes on the evidence which does exist a plausible internal consistency.

This is not to say that the opening of the enclosures, which was the immediate objective of the riot, was unimportant. The Act of 1808 had provided that the fences might be taken down after twenty-one years if the young trees were judged to be sufficiently grown to be safe from grazing animals. The first enclosures having been made in 1810, they were due to come down in 1831.[268] The Deputy Surveyor, however, had insisted that the trees were still, immature and so the Commissioners let the fences stand.[269] Miners and the other foresters had an obvious interest in opening the enclosures. This would restore 11,000 acres of pasture to them, and perhaps help to alleviate distress in the Forest. One rioter at least blamed the officers for the distress: "It's through such b...y rogues as you," he said to John Langham, the assistant to the Deputy Surveyor, "that we have no more to eat and I should like to cut your b...y head off".[270] More than this, there were signs of resentment of the curbs which the more vigorous administration of the Forest had placed on its inhabitants. Another of the rioters had said to John Hatton, a Keeper, that, "You have been our master a long while but we will let you know that we are yours now".[271] And again, from *The Forester's* explanation, the complaint that the miners:

> have been prevented from following their Mine Train through the enclosures ... in the said Forest which is contrary to (the ancient rights and privileges). Of late years they have been compelled to pay for tinnet for our hedges, fern for litter, when the above grants express that they should have the underwood free of expense, free boot and fire boot. [272]

By breaking down the fences and driving animals into the enclosures the foresters believed that they were recovering what was theirs by right; right of which they had been unjustly dispossessed by the Crown. Machen wrote after the riot that he "saw Henry and Richard Dobbs pull

268 The First Report of the Commissioners of Forests and Woods, (Session 1812) Vol.12, pp.364-365.
269 The Gloucester Journal 11 June 1831.
270 The Times 15 August 1831.
271 The Gloucester Journal 2 July 1831.
272 The Forester 4 August 1831.

away the bushes out of a gateway, and turn their cow into Cockshoot's enclosure, and when I went and expostulated them, they said they had been deprived of their rights long enough".[273] "The war word as usual", the *Merlin's* correspondent wrote, "is a restitution of rights which the foresters complain have been wrested from them by the Crown".[274] None of this is at all ambiguous: the attack on the enclosures and the campaign which preceded it constituted resistance by the miners to the extinction of their customary use rights in the Forest by 'economical reform' and the notions of the benefit of the State and the public interest which it entailed.

Apart from its other acts of oppression, the Crown was grievously at fault in "favouring foreigners who have crept in to rob us of our rights left to the miners and their heirs forever".[275] This, the magistrates had reported to the Home Office, was the rioters "most prominent ground of complaint".[276] As we have already noted, one of the rioters told K. Davies, the Monmouth banker "that they would pull up the railroads, and drive all the foreigners out of the Forest".[277] Later, while celebrating in cider the departure of the "ragged regiment" the rioters had drunk the toast: "Confusion to all foreigners".[278] On the following morning, according to James' biographer, "the order for the day was, to have up the railways, and take down the Keepers lodges and woodmen's houses erected by order of Government".[279]

As the miners, or some of them at least, saw it, the foreigners had destroyed the Mine Law Court and usurped the right to take the coal. A memorial to the Dean Forest Commissioners, signed by 1,030 people who claimed to be free miners, asserted that:

> the legality of the Mine Law Courts, and consequently the legality of their rules and regulations in all matters relating to the mines are established, and proved by the fact of their undisturbed existence, and by the exercise of their authority from times immemorial down to the year 1775, when foreigners, having obtained the discontinuance of these courts which they found to interfere with their intrusion were enabled

273 Nicholls, *The Forest of Dean*, 110.
274 *The Gloucester Journal* 11 June 1831
275 *The Forester* 4 August 1831.
276 Beaufort to the Home Office, 15 June 1831.
277 *The Gloucester Journal* 20 July 1831.
278 *The Life of Warren James*, 8.
279 Ibid, 9.

to invade their rights and violate the franchises of the free miners with impunity ... That it is the great grievance of which the free miners complain, that from their poverty they have been unable to obtain and are still prevented from obtaining, the restoration of the Mine Law Courts ... That the free miners do not anywhere pretend to deny that conveyances have been made within the last 60 years from free miners to foreigners, and that foreigners have in consequence held and worked mines openly since that period; this being the very grievance and oppression which has reduced the free miners to such distress, and proved so ruinous to the country; but they contend that this practice never could have been successfully carried on had the Mine Law Court not fallen into disuse ... The free miners therefore, most humbly entreat of Your Honourable Board to recommend the restoration of the Mine Law Courts, as the mode by which they can effectually recover their other rights and privileges, and the only step which can restore the quiet of the district, and deliver them from the oppression which they have long been suffering.[280]

As well, the foreigners, led by Protheroe and Mushet, had opposed the Purton Pill railroad proposal. They came to be seen as the operators of a pernicious monopoly which was responsible for distress in the Forest. A meeting of free miners in March 1832 at Yorkley in the Forest resolved that:

a large proportion of the Working Class of this Forest, together with their numerous Families are great Sufferers for Want of Employment; to which cause they ascribe entirely the recent Disturbances which took place in the Forest.

That at some of the most extensive Coal Works in the Forest, the Labour of the Workmen has been already reduced to Three Days per Week, (although in the middle of Winter) and the approaching Summer is likely to witness more Distress than any preceding one in consequence of the Want of Employment.

280 D.F.C., 4, p.46.

That the whole of such Distress is to be entirely ascribed to the notorious Monopoly exercised by a few Individuals in the Forest, and that the Public at large together with ourselves, are greatly injured thereby.

That if anything was required to convince the Public of the truth of this Statement, this Meeting would refer them to the WELL KNOWN FACT (established by Circular Letters from the Coalmasters of the Forest) declaring Forest Coal, conveyed along the present Lines of railway, at Bullo Pill and Lydney, at the extravagant and enormous Price of FOURTEEN SHILLINGS per Ton, although within so short a distance of the Pit's Mouth.

That under such circumstances it is impossible for the Forest to secure a Trade, (except in a few months of the year,) as the Coal from distant parts of the Kingdom is brought into our native Markets and sold at less than TEN SHILLINGS per Ton.

That nothing will open the Forest of Dean, to benefit the Public, and ensure permanent Employ to its numerous Population, short of a new Communication to Purton the old, ancient and established Shipping Port of the Forest:— where, in addition to the advantage of Home markets, the large Vessels trading to the Port of Gloucester from Ireland and other distant parts (which cannot enter the Ports of Lydney and Bullo Pill), will be supplied with a back, or outward Freight of Forest Produce; thus effectually securing the opening and working of our Mines to the Public at large, by means of the natural Port.

That it is in vain for the Proprietors and Abettors of the existing Railways to contend that the Roads already formed are adequate for such purpose or that Branches extending from their main Roads can be made beneficially applicable for the Transit of the whole of the Forest Produce. Experience has dearly taught us the contrary, and the numerous Population thrown out of Employ the greater Part of the Year, fully and lamentably demonstrates the fact. The present Railways do not afford constant Employment at the Works situated immediately upon their main Roads: And how can the produce of the Forest depend upon Branches to be united with Roads not calculated to convey their own immediate produce to market except at the enormous price we have already quoted? [281]

There was one other important grievance against the foreigners, one which affected probably the largest number of miners and brought the employed miners into an alliance with those who stood most clearly to gain from the Purton Pill scheme: "those foreigners introduced foreign miners in preference to the natives".[282] The Dean Forest Commissioners concluded that:

The claims of the free miners to the exclusive holding of gales, and to be exclusively employed as labourers to be in the mines, occasion constant and never ending jealousy and dissatisfaction on their part. The foreigners who have got into the possession of extensive works, although they in general give preference to the free miners, consider themselves quite at liberty to employ and do employ some foreign labourers. [283]

Thomas Davis, a free miner, had said in evidence to them that:

What is the grief among the miners is, that foreigners should employ foreigners instead of free miners. We should not object to foreigners, if they were obliged to employ free miners to work. I have known many free miners distressed for employment when foreigners have been in work by preference. [284]

John Worgan, another free miner, testified similarly that:

I think free miners are imposed upon very much by foreigners. They bring in their own foremen and their own foreign workmen; I was myself turned away to make room for a Bristol man, and we cannot remedy ourselves, unless our Mine Law Courts be revived. I think the Mine Law Courts would enable us to tell who was free and who was not; it would prevent foreigners managing everything their own way.[285]

281 *Resolutions of a Meeting of the Free Miners and Colliers of the Forest of Dean*, 5 March 1832.
282 *The Forester* 4 August 1831.
283. D.F.C., 4, p.9.
284 D.F.C., 4, p.7.
285 Ibid, 19.

The demand that free miners be employed exclusively did not necessarily constitute a demand that foreigners be excluded altogether. A number of those who gave evidence thought that if the foreign mine owners left the only result would be the drowning of the field and unemployment. A meeting of some of the free miners took place in April 1832. William Williams reported that:

> A great many free miners attended; much discussion took place. The general impression seemed to be, that if the foreigners had a bounty allowed for the employment of free miners in preference to foreigners, the former would be satisfied; and that the capital of the foreigners was necessary to the well being of the Forest.[286]

A considerable hostility to foreigners had thus grown up among the free miners. Distress and unemployment were the product of the monopoly which the foreigners had created by destroying the Mine Law Court and usurping the miners' rights. Not content with owning the mines, foreigners had brought other foreigners to work in the Forest. Here was a sense of injustice and of dispossession which found expression in the riot along with resentment of the State's intrusive assertion of control and its refusal to re-open the Forest. The campaign for the restoration of the Mine Law Court and the riot in which it culminated represented in sum a demand by the free miners to have control of the Forest economy returned to them, a control which miners had exercised in living memory.

Did this mean, to return to the problem with which Chapter Two closed, that the miners' demands were 'backward looking'; that the riot expressed 'social conservatism' and 'antipathy to capitalist innovation'? Did the miners wish to turn back the clock and return to the ways of living and working which had prevailed before the foreigners came and the State reasserted its control of the Forest? In the sense that the miners wished to regain an exclusive right to control the Forest's resources which they had once exercised and which had now become inoperative, the riot was backward looking. Some miners at least wished to drive away not only the foreigners and the Forest officers but the machines and railroads as well. That may be classified as backward looking. But the matter was more complex than that.

286 Ibid, 37.

Some free miners, after all, had co-operated with the foreigners since the time of James Teague's railroad. Far from resisting change they had participated in it and had attempted to turn it to their own account either by using the railroad to carry coal or taking foreigners into partnership or by acting as middlemen between the foreigners and Gaveller. The Purton Pill proposal offered new opportunity to do those same things and so to become proprietors of mines alongside a new railroad or, at the least, to register gales and sell or lease them to others. Free miner proprietors and free miner workmen stood to lose those opportunities if their exclusive rights to the minerals were abolished or the foreigners were rendered independent of the free miners. The opposition to the Bill which might have had that result should be seen not as expressing a wish to revive the old order but, on the part of some free miners, as a demand to be allowed to benefit exclusively from the new, either by doing what the foreigners had done and working mines in harness with railways or by exploiting the foreigners.

Much the same may be said of the other principal source of resentment against foreigners, the employment of foreign workmen. Some of the free miners were willing to accept foreigners as mine owners and employers but not as competitors for jobs at a time of unemployment in the Forest mines. The demand from those men to enforce the customs was a demand for exclusive employment opportunity within the altered structure of the industry. What the free miners stood to lose, as proprietors, as potential proprietors, as middlemen, and as workmen, was not the opportunity of returning to some pre-capitalist social and economic order but the means of exclusive benefit within the new system and the right to turn it to their own immediate advantage.

That is all to say that the function of the 'Laws and Customs' had altered as the free miners' economic situation had altered. In the eighteenth century, the customs had operated as a set of rules for small scale entrepreneurs. The Mine Law Court's function had been to regulate, within the broad bounds of the laws, the 'society' of small proprietors. The principal concern of the Court and its administration of the laws had been the ownership of the mineral rights. It was concerned to limit according to birth and apprenticeship the right to acquire title to the coal and then to stipulate how the proprietor should get, carry and sell the coal. But as new economic opportunities arose, free miners though not without opposition from their fellows, had given new emphasis to different parts of the Laws. Teague had justified his railroad by reference to the miners' right to make roads. He and others after him had justified taking foreigners into partnership or the sale or lease of gales to them by the clause in the Book of Dennis which allowed the miner to "bequeath and give his dole of the mine to whom he will as his of cattle". Here the emphasis was on the right to dispose of a gale as the miner wished. Others had given up without protest the right to take timber, in exchange for the use of the railroads.

By 1831 the Customs had new emphasis again. The right to exclusive title was reasserted, probably as the result of the threat from the Commissioners and the foreigners' opposition to and the opportunity offered by the Purton Pill Proposal. In addition, for the first time, the Customs were so interpreted as to be of benefit to free miners as workmen, not as proprietors or as middlemen. In both ways, the emphasis given to the Laws by some miners reflected realistically the economic situation in which they found themselves. It is thus necessary to exercise some caution in interpreting the riot, which should not simply be seen as the result of a conflict between the old system in the Forest and the new. It was a conflict primarily between free miners and intruders. Economic change had affected different free miners in different ways and it was to be expected that the ambitions and attitudes of free miners would vary accordingly. What they all had in common was that they had lost, or feared that they were about to lose, the control over their lives and the Forest's resources which were necessary to the realisation of their various ambitions.

The restoration of the Mine Law Court and the old restrictive customs would perhaps have served to restore control. But the Court had never prescribed that there should be equality among the miners, only that there should be a rough sort of equality of opportunity. Given that free miners were differently endowed in 1831 with skills, education and above all with capital and access to capital, we may suspect that capitalist productive and social relations would not have disappeared from the Forest. Nor would the machines and railroads have vanished. What is more probable is that Edward Protheroe's mantle would have passed to Moses Teague.

It seems possible now to offer some conclusions about the Dean miners' riot. It was an anti-enclosure riot, but it was a good deal more besides. Over thirty years the old system in the Forest had been transformed by economic and administrative change. Capital had penetrated the mining industry, bringing with it machines and railroads. The ownership of the mines had passed from the hands of a relatively large number of owner miners into those of a small group of men, most of whom were foreigners. In the process, the old exclusive rights of the free miners to the coal had become inoperative and the free miners had become in the main wage labourers, exposed to competition in the labour market from foreign workmen. At the same time 'economical reform' in central government had brought about a tightening of the administration of the Forest. The uses of the Forest's resources which its inhabitants had made in the eighteenth century, and had come to regard as theirs by right, were gradually curtailed and they were no longer able to build cottages, to make gardens, to take the timber and to pasture animals at will all year round. Perhaps as a matter of expediency, rather than of conspiracy, the foreign capitalists and the State had co-operated with one another and their joint and separate interests came to define the vestiges of the free miners' rights as inconvenience and anomaly.

After about 1828 the State took steps to settle finally the matter of the miners' right to get coal, in a manner which was probably intended to secure a sound legal title to their property for the foreigners. The Commissioners of Woods produced a report and a Bill which came for its second reading in the House of Commons on 20 June 1831. The miners responded by initiating a campaign designed not only to prevent further loss of rights but to restore the Mine Court and the rights which had already been lost. The riot which ran from 8 June to 12 June 1831 was probably the culmination of the miners' campaign. The riot was an expression of considerable resentment, felt by different free miners for a variety of reasons, of the intrusive State and the foreign capitalists, and it represented a demand for the restoration of the miners' old control of the Forest's resources. It is in this that the riot and the events which produced it deserve the attention of historians. The events which produced the riot are also further evidence of the displacement of customary, personal rights to the use of economic resources by the rational State and by the development of capitalist modes of industrial organisation and the notions of property inherent in them. The riot was symptomatic of the resentment felt by those who were dispossessed in the making of the new system.

It remains only to record by way of terse epilogue that the Commissioners' Bill was read and in due course, the Dean Forest (Commission) Act passed on to the Statute Books.[287] There followed ten years of inquiry, of reports, of further inquiry and further reports and a series of Acts of Parliament. In sum, this process clearly established the

---

287 1 and 2 Will. IV, c.12.

title and rights of the State in the land, timber and minerals. The problem of the free miners' rights was settled by the Dean Forest (Mines) Act of 1838.[288] This Act defined and confirmed the free miners' rights and appointed yet another Commission to establish the boundaries of the existing mines. On the face of it, this statutory recognition of the rights was a great victory for the free miners. Clause(e) of the Act read in part:

> Registered free miners to have the exclusive right of having gales or works granted to them.

The Mining Commissioners presented the Act in its most favourable light to a meeting of free miners at the opening of the Commission in September 1838:

> An ancient privilege has been perpetuated from time to time, and one of the first objects contemplated by the Act, is to establish that privilege on a firmer and broader basis than it has hitherto existed. The basis is firmer in as much as it has the direct recognition of Parliament, not merely to the vague and indefinite right of galing, but to the possession of a definite tract of forest coal. It is firmer also, because the transfer of his mining property has in former times been subject to some doubt and uncertainty; whereas, it is now placed fully and fairly within the legitimate disposal of every free miner. It is established on a firmer basis also, inasmuch as all doubt is removed as to who are now to be considered free miners; and a registry is provided which will prevent all doubt in future on that score.[289]

But what was this victory worth? A free miner was defined by the Act as:

> All male persons born or hereafter to be born and abiding within the said Hundred of Saint Briavels, at the age of twenty-one years and upwards, who shall have worked a year and a day in a coal or iron mine within the said Hundred of Saint Briavels, shall be deemed and taken to be free miners for the purposes of this act.

288 1 and 2 Vict., c.43.
289 T Sopwith, *Observations addressed to a Public Meeting the Free Miners*, 5 September 1838, 3.

The critical Qualification of the old definition, that a free miner had to be the son of a free miner, had disappeared. There was no provision that only free miners be employed in the mines. Moreover, Clause (10) of the Act stipulated that:

> Registered free miners may sell, transfer, assign or dispose of such gales, works or quarries by deed or will, to each other, or to any other party.

As well, Clause (21) confirmed all mortgages, leases and sales made prior to the Act. In other words, the Act gave the foreigners clear title, confirmed their right to employ men other than free miners and gave legislative sanction to the process of sale and lease by which they had acquired the mines in the first place. The operative principle in the Act, as the Mining Commissioners pointed out, was the recognition of property rights. Whatever doubt hung over the foreigners' title:

> as regards its origin, or as regards its being an encroachment on the customs, is fully set at rest by the Act, which recognises them as being now proprietors of mines, and entitled to a full enjoyment of that property according to the particular circumstances of each case … While, therefore, the rights of the free miner are not only recognised but confirmed and increased, it is due to common justice and to English fairness and uprightness, that the general rights of property shall be respected; this has been our object and it forms a distinguishing, and I have no doubt, when properly considered and understood, a highly popular, feature of the present Act. [290]

At the same time, the qualification for freedom was left so open as to be, in the long run, worthless. What this remarkable Act gave with one hand it dexterously whipped away with the other. In the year that the Mines Act became law, his Majesty pardoned Warren James; but no news of or from him ever came back to the Forest.[291]

290 Ibid, 4–5.
291 Nicholls, *Forest of Dean*, 12.

Bibliography

Public Record Office

Assizes 1: Minute Book, 1831.

Assizes 6: Depositions, 1831-35.

Crest 8/1-18: Early Treasury Letter Books, 1803-1831.

Crest 9/1-26: England and Country, Letter Books and Treasury Report Books, 1802-1832.

Crest 22/1-7: Solicitor's Department, Letter Book, 1812-1832.

Crest 25/1-35: Minute Book of the Commissioners of Woods, 1803-31.

Crest 40/62-65: Commissioners of Woods, Forests and Land Revenues Letter Books, 1786-1793.

F3/5: Establishment: Retirement of Deputy Surveyor Machen, 1853-4.

F3/145: Verderers Courts, Proceedings etc., 1829-1860.

F3/226: Awards of Mining Commissioners, 1835-71.

F3/234: Severn and Wye Railway.

F3/263: Common Rights.

F3/608: Cinderford Iron Works, 1827-1901.

F3/724: Maps, Plans and Surveys, 1786-1909.

F3/837: Preparation of the Dean Forest (Mines) Act, 1836-47.

F3/893: Proposed Railway from Purton-on-Severn, 1828-1904.

F16/31: Particulars of a Survey of the Forest of Dean undertaken by William and Abraham Driver.

F16/33: Railway Acts relating to the Forest.

F16/34: Correspondence relating to the making of Railways and Tramways in the Forest.

F17/426: Plans of the Coal and Iron Mine Districts of the Forest with a manuscript copy of the Mining Commissioners' Award of Coal Mines, 1841.

F20/2: Mining Claims and Disputes: details of encroachments, depredations and abuses in the Forest, 1805.

F20/6: Minute Book of the Proceedings of the Commissioners John Puddle, John Probyn and Thomas Sopwith, 1838-40.

F20/7: Depositions and other evidences as to the rights of mines laid before the Mining Commissioners at their inquiry.

F20/8-10; Claims to gales and mine workings inquired into by the Commissioners, and evidence heard by them, 1839-40.

H.O. 40/27 and 29: Disturbances, Correspondence and Papers.

H.O. 41/10: Disturbances, Entry Books, 1831.

H.O. 44/24: Domestic, George IV and later, 1831.

H.O. 43/39-40: Domestic Letter Books, July 1830 - November 1831.

H.O. 52/12: Counties Correspondence, Berks - Gloucester, 1831.

T 25/1-15: Treasury Out Letters, Woods and Forests. 1773-1831.

Newspapers and Periodicals

Cobbett's Weekly Political Register 1831.
Gloucester Herald 1827-1828.
Gloucester Journal 1800-1831.
Gloucester Mercury 1828-1829.
Monmouthshire Merlin 1829-1831.
The Forester 1831.
The Times 1831.

Dissertations

Amos, S.W. *Agrarian Disturbances in Essex. 1790 - 1850*, M.A., Durham, 1971.
Colson, A. M. *The Revolt of the Hampshire Agricultural Labourers and its Causes 1812 - 1831*, M.A., London, 1937.
Dutt, M. *The Agricultural Labourers' Revolt of 1830 in Kent, Surrey and Sussex*, Ph.D., London, 1966.
Gash, N.G. *The Rural Unrest in England in 1830 with particular reference to Berkshire*, B.Litt., Oxford, 1934.

Official Publications

Local and Personal Acts.
Parliamentary Debates 1829-1831.
Parliamentary Papers.
Reports of the Commissioners appointed to inquire into the state and condition of the Woods, Forests and Land Revenues of the Crown, I-XVII, 1787-1793.
Reports of the Surveyor General of His Majesty's Land Revenue, I – IV, 1797-1809.
Reports of the Commissioners of Woods and Forests, I – VIII, 1812-31.
Reports of the Dean Forest Commissioners, 1-V, 1835.
Return from the Commissioners of Woods and Forests of Information respecting the Mines in Dean Forest, 1818.
Report of the Commissioners of Woods and Forests recommending measures for ascertaining the Boundaries of Dean Forest, and for Inquiry into the Rights or Claims of Persons calling themselves Free Miners, 1829.
A Bill for Ascertaining the Boundaries of the Forest of Dean, and inquiry into the Rights and Privileges claimed by the Free Miners of the Hundred of St Briavels, and for other purpose, 1830.
Reports of the Dean Forest Mining Commissioners, I - III, 1839-41.
Population Abstracts, 1801-1831.
Public General Acts.
The Statutes of the Realm.

Books, Articles and. Pamphlets

Addis, John P. *The Crawshay Dynasty: A Study in Industrial Organization and Development, 1765-1867*, Cardiff: University of Wales Press, 1957.

Albion, E.G. *Forests and Sea Power 1652-1862*, Harvard Economic Studies, XXIX, 1926.

Aldcroft, D.H. and Pearson, P. (eds), *British Economic Fluctuations 1790 -1939*, 1972.

Ashton, T.S. *The Industrial Revolution*, Oxford: Oxford University Press, 1948.

Ashton, T.S. *Economic Fluctuations in England 1700-1800*, Oxford: Clarendon Press, 1959.

Ashton, T.S. and Sykes, J. *The Coal Industry of the Eighteenth Century*, Manchester: Manchester University Press, 1929.

Bellows, J. Relics of Ancient British Forest Life, *Transactions of Bristol & Gloucestershire Archaeological Society*, Volume 6, 1881-2.

Beveridge, W. H. *The Trade Cycle in Britain Before 1850*, Oxford Economic Papers, Volume 3, 1940.

Beveridge, W. H. *The Trade Cycle in Britain Before 1850: A Postscript*, Oxford Economic Papers, 4, 1940.

Brook, M. *The Great Reform Act*, London: Hutchinson, 1973.

Chambers, J.D. and Mingay, G.E. *The Agricultural Revolution, 1750 - 1880*, London: Badsford, 1966.

Checkland, S.G. *The Rise of Industrial Society in England, 1815 - 1885*, London: Longman, 1964.

Cole, G.D.H. and Postgate, R. *The Common People 1746 - 1946*, 9th ed., London: Methuen, 1966.

Cooke, A.C. *The Forest of Dean*, London: Constable, 1913.

Cooper, W. The Laws and Customs of the Miners in the Forest of Dean in *The Compleat Miner*, 1688.

Cox, J.C. *Royal Forests of England*, London: Methuen, 1905.

Crawley Boevey, S.M. *Dean Forest Sketches*, John and Robert Maxwell, 1887.

Cross, A.L. Eighteenth Century Documents relating to the Royal Forests, *The American Historical Review*, Volume 34, Issue 1, October 1928, 119–120.

Deane, P. *The First Industrial Revolution*, New York: Cambridge University Press, 1965.

Deane, P. and Cole, W.A. *British Economic Growth 1688 -1959*, New York: Cambridge University Press, 1969.

Dobb, M. *Studies in the Development of Capitalism* (Rev. edition, 1949) 244.

Einzig, P. *The Control of the Purse*, London: Secker & Warburg, 1959.

Galloway, R.L. *A History of Coal Mining in Great Britain*, Revised ed., Newton Abbot: David & Charles, 1969.

Galloway, R.L. *Annals of Coal Mining and The Coal Trade*, 2 Vols., Newton Abbot: David & Charles, 1971.

Gayer, A.D., Rostow, W.W. and Schwartz, A.J. *The Growth and Fluctuation of the British Economy,* 2 Vols., Oxford: Clarendon, 1953.

Gurr, T.R. *Why Men Rebel,* 4th ed., Princetown: Princetown University Press, 1972.

Hammond, J.L. The Industrial Revolution and Discontent, *Economic History Review,* Vol. 2, No. 2, 1930.

Hammond, J.L. and B. *The Rise of Modern Industry,* 2nd ed., London: Methuen, 1926.

Hammond, J.L. and B. *The Village Labourer,* 2 vols., 10th ed., London: Longmans, 1948.

Hammond, J.L. and B. *The Town Labourer,* 2 vols., 11th ed., London: Longmans, 1949.

Hart, C.E. *The Extent of the Boundaries of the Forest of Dean,* 1947.

Hart, C.E. *The Verderers and the Speech Court of the Forest of Dean,* Gloucester: Bellows, 1950.

Hart, C.E. *The Commoners of Dean Forest,* Gloucester: British Publishing Company, 1951.

Hart, C.E. *Laws of Dean,* 1952.

Hart, C.E. *The Free Miners of the Forest of Dean,* Gloucester: British Publishing Company, 1953.

Hart, C.E. *The Industrial History of Dean,* Newton Abbot, David and Charles, 1971.

Hart, C.E. *The Royal Forest,* Oxford: Clarendon, 1966.

Hart, C.E. (ed.) *Nicholls' Forest of Dean,* Newton Abbot: David and Charles, 1966.

Heath, C. *Historical and Descriptive Account of Chepstow and neighbourhood,* Monmouth, 6th ed., 1813.

Hibbert, C. *King Mob,* London: Reader's Union, 1958.

Hobsbawm, E.J. *Labouring Men* 3rd ed., London: Weidenfeld and Nicolson 1968.

Hobsbawm, E.J. *Industry and Empire,* London: Weidenfeld and Nicolson, 1968.

Hobsbawm, E.J. *Primitive Rebels* 4th ed., Manchester: Manchester University Press, 1974.

Hobsbawm, E.J. and Rude, G, *Captain Swing* Rev. ed., London: Penguin, 1973.

Hoffmann, W.G. *British industry* 1700 - 1950, Oxford: Blackwell, 1955.

Inglis, B. *Poverty and the Industrial Revolution,* London: Hodder & Stoughton, 1971.

Jevons, William Stanley, *The Coal Question; An Inquiry Concerning the Progress of the Nation, and the Probable Exhaustion of Our Coal Mines,* 2nd ed., London: Macmillan, 1906.

John, A.H. *The Industrial Development of South Wales,* Cardiff: Cardiff University Press, 1950.

Jones, D. *Before Rebecca,* London: Allen Lane, 1973.

Kemp, B. *King and Commons, 1660-1872,* London: Macmillan, 1959.

Kerr, R. J. The Customs of the Forest of Dean, *Transactions of Bristol & Gloucestershire Archaeological Society,* Vol. 43, 63-78, 1921.

Mathias, P. *The First Industrial Nation,* London: Methuen, 1969.

Muir, E. *Local Government in Gloucestershire,* 1775 -1800, Bristol, 1969.

Mountjoy, T. *Sixty-two Years in the Life of a Forest of Dean Collier,* 1867.

Nef, J.U. *The Rise of the British Coal Industry* 2 vols., Rev. ed., London: Routledge, 1966.

Nicholls, H.G. *The Personalities of the Forest of Dean,* London: John Murray, 1863.

Nicholls, H.G. *The Forest of Dean,* 2nd edition, edited by C.E. Hart, Whitstable: David and Charles, 1966, 1st edition 1858.

Nisbet, J. History of the Forest of Dean in Gloucestershire, *English Historical Review,* Volume, 1906.

Osborn, F.M. *The Story of the Mushets,* London: Nelson, 1952.

Paar, H.W. *The Severn and Wye Railway,* 2nd ed, Newton Abbot: David and Charles, 1973.

Paar, H.W. *The Great Western Railway in Dean,* 2nd. ed, Newton Abbot, David and Charles, 1971.

Peacock, A.J. *Bread on Blood. The Agrarian Riots in East Anglia 1816,* London: Victor Gollancz, 1965.

Perkin, H. *The Origins of Modern British Society,* 1780 - 1880, London: Routledge and Kegan Paul, 1969.

Pollard, S. and Crossley, D.W. *The Wealth of Britain,* London: Batsford, 1968.

Resident Forester, *The Life of Warren James, The Reputed Champion of The Forest of Dean, Descriptive of the Forest Riots, including an Account of John Harris Alias Poisefoot,* Monmouth: Heath, 1831.

Rosaveare, H. *The Treasury, 1660 -1870,* Unwin, 1973.

Rude, G. *The Crowd in the French Revolution,* Oxford: Oxford University Press, 1959.

Rude, G. *The Crowd in History,* New York: Wiley, 1964.

Rude, G. English Rural and Urban Disturbances on the Eve of the First Reform Bill, 1830-31, *Past and Present,* 37, 1967.

Shaw, Lefevre G. *English Commons and Forests,* London: Cassell, 1894.

Silby, T.F. *The Haematites of the Forest of Dean and South Wales,* London: HMSO, 1927.

Smelsen, N. J. *Social Change and the Industrial Revolution,* London: Routledge and Kegan Paul, 1959.

Sopwith, T. *Observations addressed to a public meeting of the Free Miners,* C. Roworth, 1838.

Stevenson, J. and Quinault, R. *Popular Protest and Public Order,* London: Allen and Unwin, 1974.

Sweezy, P. M. *Monopoly Competition in the English Coal Trade: 1550-1850*, 2nd ed., Cambridge: Harvard University Press, 1972.

Tate, W.E. *The English Village Community and the Enclosure Movements*, London: Victor Gollancz, 1967.

Taylor, A. J. (ed.) *The Standard of Living in Britain in the Industrial Revolution*, London: Methuen, 1975.

Thompson, E. P. English Trade Unionism and Other Labour Movements Before 1790, *Society for the Study of Labour History*, Bulletin, Autumn, 1968.

Thompson, E. P. *The Making of the English Working Class*, Rev. ed., Middlesex: Penguin 1968.

Thompson, E. P. The Moral Economy of the English Crowd in the Eighteenth Century, *Past and Present*, No 50, 1971.

Thompson, E. P. Patrician Society, Plebeian Culture, *Journal of Social History*, Summer, 1974.

Tiny, C. Collective Violence in European Perspective, in Graham, H.D. and Garr, T.H. (eds), *Violence in America*, Historical and Comparative Perspectives, Washington: US Government, 1969.

Tilly, C., Tilly, L. and Tilly, R. *The Rebellious Century, 1830 - 1930*, Cambridge Mass: Harvard University Press, 1975.

Townley, H. *English Woodlands and their Story*, London: Methuen, 1910.

Trotter, F.M. *Geology of the Forest of Dean Coal and Iron-ore Field*, London: HMSO, 1942.

Wearmouth, R. F. *Methodism and the Common People of the Eighteenth Century*, London: Epworth Press, 1945.

Wearmouth, R. F. *Methodism and the Working, Class Movements of England 1800 -1850* 2nd edition, London: Epworth Press, 1947.

Williams, R. *The Country and the City*, Oxford: Oxford University Press, 1973.

The Free Miners of Dean Forest, Penny Magazine, 19 August 1843.

110

Acknowledgements

First of all, thanks to Chris Fisher who kindly agreed to allow Bristol Radical History Group to publish his dissertation. Chris started his working life as a miner and ended up as a sheep and grain farmer. Therefore, as a keen fan of rugby, Chris has much in common with many Foresters. Thanks also to Richard Musgrove, Lynda Mansell and Hedley Bashforth for proof reading and to Richard Grove for design and layout.

The acknowledgements in the original dissertation are given by Chris as follows:

I wish to thank the staff of the Social History Centre for their guidance in the preparation of this paper. Thanks are particularly due to Fred Reid and Allan Campbell, my supervisors, for their advice and criticism. Errors of fact, judgement and taste in the paper remain, of course, my own responsibility. I am also grateful for the patient assistance of staff in a number of libraries: the University of Warwick Library, the British Library, the Newspaper Library at Colindale, the Public Records Office, the Gloucester Public Library and the County Records Office in Gloucester. I am grateful too to Mrs A. Perrot for her help with the typing. My debt is especially great to my wife for long, hard labour at the typewriter and for the support and help she has given me in so many other ways.

The front cover is adapted from the frontispiece of H. G. Nicholls, *The Forest of Dean: An Historical and Descriptive Account* (London: Murray, 1858). It depicts two Forest of Dean iron miners from the 1830s with a candle holder made from clay, called a nellie, to help them see in the dark. They held the nellie in their mouths so they could work with both hands. Forest mines do not have methane gas so it was safe to use naked flames.